Criminal Justice
Recent Scholarship

Edited by
Nicholas P. Lovrich

A Series from LFB Scholarly

The Anti-Social Network
Cyberstalking Victimization among College Students

Bradford W. Reyns

LFB Scholarly Publishing LLC
El Paso 2012

Copyright © 2012 by LFB Scholarly Publishing LLC

All rights reserved.

Library of Congress Cataloging-in-Publication Data

Reyns, Bradford W., 1979-
 The anti-social network : cyberstalking victimization among college students / Bradford W. Reyns.
   p. cm.
 Includes bibliographical references and index.
 ISBN 978-1-59332-538-1 (hardcover : alk. paper)
 1. Cyberstalking. 2. Computers and college students. I. Title.
 HV6773.15.C94R49 2012
 364.15'8--dc23
                              2012021391

ISBN 978-1-59332-538-1

Printed on acid-free 250-year-life paper.

Manufactured in the United States of America.

Table of Contents

List of Tables vii

List of Figures ix

Chapter 1: The Problem of Cyberstalking 1

Chapter 2: Lifestyle-Routine Activities Theory 29

Chapter 3: The Theoretical Transition to Cyberspace 45

Chapter 4: Researching the Problem of Cyberstalking 59

Chapter 5: The Extent and Nature of Cyberstalking Victimization 81

Chapter 6: Summary, Implications, and the Future of
     Cyberstalking Research 111

Appendices 129

References 177

Index 193

List of Tables

Table 1.1: Summary of Cyberstalking Victimization (CSV) Studies 20

Table 4.1: Select Sample and Population Characteristics 64

Table 4.2: Cyberstalking and Identity Fraud Victimization Variables 68

Table 4.3: Online Exposure Variables 69

Table 4.4: Online Guardianship Variables 70

Table 4.5: Online Proximity Variables 71

Table 4.6: Online Target Attractiveness Variables 73

Table 4.7: Online Deviance Variables 74

Table 4.8: Self-Control Survey Items 76

Table 5.1: Extent of Victimization by Demographics and Type of Online Victimization[a] 85

Table 5.2: Percentage and Number of Males and Females Victimized[a] in Lifetime by Select Demographic Characteristics 86

Table 5.3: Bivariate Relationships[a] between Independent Variables and Control Variables 90

Table 5.4: Bivariate Relationships[a] between Independent/Control Variables and Victimization Variables 92

Table 5.5: Binary Logistic Regression Coefficients, Standard Errors, and Exponentiated Coefficients for Unwanted Contact 100

Table 5.6: Binary Logistic Regression Coefficients, Standard Errors, and Exponentiated Coefficients for Online Harassment 101

Table 5.7: Binary Logistic Regression Coefficients, Standard Errors, and Exponentiated Coefficients for Sexual Advances 102

Table 5.8: Binary Logistic Regression Coefficients, Standard Errors, and Exponentiated Coefficients for Threats of Violence 103

Table 5.9: Binary Logistic Regression Coefficients, Standard Errors, and Exponentiated Coefficients for Overall Cyberstalking Victimization 104

Table 5.10: Binary Logistic Regression Coefficients, Standard Errors, and Exponentiated Coefficients for Identity Fraud 105

Table 5.11: Summary of Lifestyle-Routine Activities Findings for Cyberstalking Victimization 109

Table 6.1: Using Situational Crime Prevention to Limit Opportunities for Cyberstalking 123

List of Figures

Figure 2.1: The Lifestyle-Exposure Theoretical Model of Personal Victimization 35

Figure 2.2: The Crime Triangle 36

Figure 3.1: The Transition from Places to Networks 47

Figure 3.2: Routine Activities in an Online Domain 47

Figure 5.1: Percentage of Respondents who Experienced Online Victimization 82

Figure 6.1: The Asynchronous Intersection of Victims and Offenders in Online Environments 121

Figure 6.2: The New Crime Triangle 124

CHAPTER 1
The Problem of Cyberstalking

VICTIMIZATION

Despite the fact that every crime has a victim, criminologists have focused almost exclusively on offenders for most of the discipline's history. It was not until about halfway through the twentieth century that the first generation of victimologists began to devote research attention to victim-centered issues. The scientific study of victims can be traced back to the work of several scholars, including von Hentig (1948), Wolfgang (1958), Schafer (1968), Amir (1971), and Mendelsohn (1976), who each in their own way proposed that victims were responsible to some degree for their victimization. In time, the field of victimology expanded in scope to explain not only the victim's role in their victimization, but other aspects of victimization as well (e.g., correlates, consequences) (see Doerner, 2010; Fisher & Reyns, 2009). Subsequent generations of victimologists have called attention to the importance of opportunity as a precursor to victimization (e.g., Cohen & Felson, 1979; Hindelang, Gottfredson, & Garofalo, 1978; Wilcox, Land, & Hunt, 2003). It is in the work of these scholars and those that followed them that the current study is grounded.

The advent of the National Crime Survey (NCS) in 1972 and other subsequent victim surveys (e.g., British Crime Survey, National Violence Against Women Survey, National Victimization Against College Women Surveys) greatly expanded the research capabilities of victimologists by providing much needed data for testing and refining theories. Since that time, victimologists have explored a variety of types of victimization, ranging from broad categories (i.e., personal, property) to particular types (e.g., rape, larceny, stalking), and considered the victimization experiences of a number of specific populations (e.g., college students, adolescents, adults). In this tradition, the focus of this study is the cyberstalking victimization of college students.

CYBERVICTIMIZATION

The advent of the Internet and the resulting ability to acquire information and communicate with persons across the globe has fundamentally changed our world. The importance of these technological changes cannot be overstated; these technological changes have had reverberations in every aspect of our lives from business, to art and culture, to dating and social networking. Along with these advancements in technology have come a new supply of criminal opportunities and a seemingly endless source of victims (Clarke, 2004; Grabosky, 2007; Newman & Clarke, 2003; Reyns, 2010; Wall, 2008). The criminal opportunities produced in cyberspace have opened up a whole new category of crime for criminologists to study—*cybercrimes*. As with all types of crime, different opportunity structures facilitate the occurrence of cybercrimes. While it is true that in general all cybercrimes require a network to connect offenders with victims, the tactics, methods, motivations, and consequences of cybercrime victimizations vary across types of cybercrimes. Online networks connect people and organizations all over the world, and it is this connection that has facilitated both entirely new types of crimes (e.g., computer hacking) and created online counterparts to existing crimes (e.g., fraud, stalking, bullying). These online counterparts are essentially a "version 2.0" for many types of traditional crimes. In addition to fraud, stalking, and bullying, other behaviors such as harassment, sex offenses, various types of organized crimes, and even terrorism have adapted to cyberspace. Some of these crimes are essentially extensions of their offline counterparts, while others are similar in some ways, but different in others; such is the case with cyberstalking.

Cybercrimes offer criminologists and victimologists new territory in which to examine the etiology of crime and victimization, as well as fertile ground for testing and refining current criminological and victimological theories. However, despite this, few cybercrimes have been rigorously studied, and still fewer studies have examined cyberstalking. This study is an attempt to address this theoretical and empirical shortfall, and to provide a more inclusive and methodologically solid estimate of the extent and nature of cyberstalking victimization. To this end, the purposes of this study are threefold: (1) to estimate the extent of cyberstalking victimization among a sample of college students from a large urban university in the Midwest; (2) to utilize the lifestyle-exposure and routine activity theory perspectives (LRAT) in order determine the correlates and risk factors for cyberstalking victimization; and, (3) to assess whether the lifestyle-routine activities perspective can be adapted to explain victimization in virtual environments. Implications for crime prevention and the future of cyberstalking research will also be discussed.

THE STALKING AND CYBERSTALKING OF COLLEGE STUDENTS

Stalking and Cyberstalking

According to Fisher and Stewart (2007: 211), being stalked involves being "repeatedly pursued in a manner that causes a reasonable person to fear for his or her safety." This is a definition that is consistent with anti-stalking statutes and much of the extant research on stalking victimization. There are two key components of this definition – one behavioral and the other emotional. The behavioral aspect of stalking is the *repeated pursuit* behaviors the victim experiences, and the emotional aspect is the harm suffered by the victim in the form of *fear*. Other conceptions of stalking may not include the victim's fear, instead using words such as "emotional distress," "annoyance," or "harassment" to describe the harm experienced by the victim as a result of the pursuit behaviors. With respect to anti-stalking laws, the fear criteria are typically met if the victim reasonably feared for their safety or the safety of an immediate family member as a result of the pursuit. Behaviors are usually considered to be repeated if they have occurred on two or more occasions. Other researchers have employed more strict criteria before labeling an incident as stalking. For instance, Sheridan and Grant (2007), consistent with Pathé, Mullen, and Purcell's (2000) criteria for repetition and persistence, considered the offense of stalking/cyberstalking to have occurred only if the pursuit behaviors lasted for four or more weeks and occurred on ten or more occasions. Regardless of the definition used, studies consistently find that stalking is experienced by a significant number of victims (e.g., Baum, Catalano, Rand, & Rose, 2009; Bjerregaard, 2000; Buhi, Clayton, & Surrency, 2009; Cupach & Spitzberg, 2004; Davis & Frieze, 2002; Fisher, Cullen, & Turner, 2000, 2002; Fisher, Daigle, & Cullen, 2010a; Jordan, Wilcox, & Pritchard, 2007; Nobles, Fox, Piquero, & Piquero, 2009; Wilcox, Jordan, & Pritchard, 2007).

While "traditional" physically proximal stalking (that is, stalking that occurs in spatial proximity to the victim) has received quite a bit of research attention over the last decade (e.g., Cupach & Spitzberg, 2004; Davis & Frieze, 2002; Fisher, 2001; Fisher et al., 2002; Mustaine & Tewksbury, 1999; Tjaden & Thonnes, 1998), its online counterpart has been comparatively neglected by researchers. Cyberstalking is a crime of relatively recent vintage, with the first recorded incident occurring in the late 1990s[1] (Henson, 2010; McQuade, 2006). It is also a crime that is not well understood. Although the lay person may have some vague conception of what cyberstalking involves, few understand its intricacies. Indeed, there has been a "growing process" among legislators, academics, law enforcement professionals, and others in determining exactly what cyberstalking entails.

Cyberstalking[2] is a crime of repeated pursuit utilizing electronic communications to do any or all of the following behaviors on two or more occasions: contacting someone after being asked to stop; harassing, annoying or tormenting someone; making unwanted sexual advances toward someone; and communicating threats of physical

---

[1] Estimates vary as to when the first incident and prosecution of cyberstalking occurred (Henson, 2010; McQuade, 2006).

[2] Just as there is no consistent definition of cyberstalking or stalking in the extant literature, there is also no consensus as to which terms are used when discussing these types of victimization. Stalking is often simply called stalking, unless it is being discussed in the same realm as cyberstalking, in which case it is often referred to as proximal, offline, spatial, traditional, terrestrial, or conventional stalking. For the sake of consistency, stalking will either be referred to as simply *stalking* or *physically proximal stalking*. Similarly, cyberstalking is often called *online stalking*. Further, some authors separate and/or hyphenate cyberstalking (i.e., cyber-stalking, cyber stalking). Again, for the sake of consistency, *cyberstalking* will be the only term assigned to such behavior throughout this study.

violence against someone (Henson, 2010). It has also been suggested that behaviors such as identity fraud, data theft, hacking, and damage to computer equipment are forms of cyberstalking (e.g., Bocij, 2003). Each of these online behaviors has been facilitated by technological innovations that freed potential stalkers of the spatial restrictions of their repeated pursuit behaviors.

As noted, in comparison to the methodologically rigorous work with stalking, relatively few studies have focused exclusively upon cyberstalking. Most of these have been methodologically weak in some way, relying on convenience samples, employing small sample sizes, and using ambiguous measures of cyberstalking victimization (Yar, 2006). This may account for why estimates of the extent of victimization have been so varied. Further, few of these early studies of cyberstalking victimization have been guided by theory. To date, only a handful of studies have utilized the lifestyle-routine activities approach to identify risk factors for victimization, but the dependent variables in these studies were operationalized using only one of the com-component behaviors of cyberstalking (i.e., online harassment) (Bossler & Holt, 2010; Bossler, Holt, & May, 2011; Holt & Bossler, 2009; Marcum, Higgins, & Ricketts, 2010). The paucity of work focused on cybercrimes, and cyberstalking specifically, has made it difficult to devise prevention strategies. This is not for lack of crime prevention or victimological theory. Environmental criminology in particular has a wealth of theories (e.g., crime pattern theory, rational choice theory, routine activities theory) that have the potential of expanding our understanding of cybercrimes. A greater knowledge of different types of cybercrime, including cyberstalking, and their respective opportunity structures will aid researchers and practitioners in developing crime prevention strategies.

Defining Cyberstalking
Part of the challenge in studying cyberstalking has been in determining exactly what the phenomenon entails (e.g., Bocij, 2006; Bocij & McFarlane, 2002b). There is no universally accepted definition of cyberstalking; however, there is a consensus that stalkers carry out pur-

suit of their victims by means of some type of telecommunications device or via the Internet (e.g., through emails, text messages, faxes) (Ashcroft, 2001; Bocij & McFarlane, 2002a, 2002b; D'Ovidio & Doyle, 2003; Levrant Miceli, Santana, & Fisher, 2001; Maxwell, 2001; Reno, 1999). There is also little agreement regarding whether cyberstalking is different than physically proximal stalking, and this distinction becomes even more difficult to make when a stalker pursues his victim both online in cyberspace and in physical proximity (Bocij, 2006; Bocij & McFarlane, 2003b; Henson, 2010; Parsons-Pollard & Moriarty, 2008; Pittaro, 2008; Reyns & Englebrecht, 2010; Sheridan & Grant, 2007).

Legal definitions of stalking and cyberstalking vary by state and country (Fox, Nobles, & Fisher, 2011; Tjaden, 2009). California, for instance, requires three criteria for stalking (that also cover cyberstalking): (1) the victim can prove a pattern of conduct on the part of the stalker that was intended to alarm or harass; (2) as a result of this pursuit, the victim reasonably feared for their safety or the safety of their immediate family; and, (3) the stalker either made a credible threat against the victim or violated a restraining order. California law also stipulates that the victim demand the stalker cease their pursuit of the victim. Massachusetts law has a less stringent definition of stalking, defining it as (1) a pattern of conduct which the victim finds severely annoying or alarming that (2) also includes a threat to bodily injury or intent to instill fear of death. In general, state laws emphasize the repeated nature of communication directed at the victim, some consequence of the pursuit (e.g., annoyance, fear, distress), and a threat of physical harm.

There is no federal cyberstalking law per se, but certain federal laws such as 18 U.S.C. 875(c) (which prohibits threatening communication), 47 U.S.C. 223 (which proscribes the use of telecommunication devices to harass, threaten, annoy, or abuse someone anonymously), and the amended Violence Against Women Act (1994, 2005) all prohibit cyberstalking at the federal level. National-level legislation covering cyberstalking also exists in other countries. Australia, for instance, defines unlawful stalking conduct as: (1) intentionally directed at a person; (2) occurring on more than one occasion; and, (3) consisting of one or more of a number of specific acts (including contacting a person by email, phone, fax, mail, or though any other technology).

Based on state and federal laws prohibiting stalking and cyberstalking, as well as definitions of cyberstalking used in prior research, the behaviors comprising cyberstalking victimization were identified for use in the current study. The four components of cyberstalking victimization include: (1) repeatedly being contacted after asking the other person to stop; (2) receiving communications that are perceived by the victim to be harassing, annoying, or tormenting; (3) receiving unwanted sexual advances; and, (4) receiving threats of physical violence (Bocij, 2003, 2006; Bocij & McFarlane, 2002b; Finn, 2004; Henson, 2010; Parsons-Pollard & Moriarty, 2008). It has also been suggested that having one's identity stolen[3] and/or assumed with intent to do damage may be a form of cyberstalking victimization. Cyberstalking, therefore, can involve multiple pursuit behaviors that separately or in conjunction constitute cyberstalking victimization. This includes receiving any one of the four specific forms of online communication by another Internet user or users on two or more occasions. Not only must these attempts at communication be repeated, but they must serve no legitimate purpose (e.g., the purpose it to harass or annoy the victim).

The components of this definition were identified over the years as legislators, researchers, and law enforcement professionals grappled with defining the techniques and behaviors that comprise this new type of crime. Despite these advances, there is no universally accepted defi-

---

[3] The inclusion of identity theft on this list is arguable. Cyberstalkers have been known to hack their victim's email clients or social networks, pose as their victim, and otherwise try to bring harm on the victim by assuming their identty. These behaviors, however, do not necessarily need to be repeated two or more times before the incident can be labeled as cyberstalking. Further, the label *identity theft* while technically not inaccurate in this context is somewhat mileading, as it carries certain connotations (e.g., identity theft for monetary gain). For this reason, perhaps a more appropriate label may be *identity fraud* (Koops & Leenes, 2006; Reyns, 2011; Taylor, Fritsch, Liederbach & Holt, 2010), which can encompass a host of criminal behaviors that can occur online involving the theft of personal information.

nition of cyberstalking in the research community. The above definition is used in this study to define cyberstalking, and is based on anti-stalking statutes and previous research. This definition is consistent with the definition developed by Bocij and McFarlane (2002b: 12), who defined cyberstalking as:

> "A group of behaviours in which an individual, group of individuals or organization, uses information and communications technology to harass one or more individuals. Such behaviours may include, but are not limited to, the transmission of threats and false accusations, identity theft, data theft, damage to data or equipment, computer monitoring, the solicitation of minors for sexual purposes and confrontation."

Fear of Victimization
Noteworthy is that absent from either of these definitions[4] is any mention of the fear felt by the victim. Is victim fear a prerequisite for an incident to be labeled cyberstalking? This is a further point of conceptual uncertainty among scholars studying cyberstalking. Indeed, many state laws governing cyberstalking do not make mention of fear. State laws vary in their cyberstalking legislation, with some states having specific cyberstalking statutes, others relying on stalking statutes, and others prosecuting cyberstalking with general harassment statutes. As Appendix 1 illustrates, most states make some mention of fear in their harassment or stalking statutes. However, a majority do not require the victim to feel fear for stalking or cyberstalking to have legally occurred.

Currently, it is the case that researchers, legislators, and law enforcement professionals know too little about the phenomenon of cyberstalking or feelings of fear generated by online encounters to make a determination that cyberstalking requires an emotional response from the victim (e.g., fear). Consider the following example: an individual receives repeated threats of violence, harassing emails, and their name is used in ways that are meant to tarnish it, but the victim never experiences fear (perhaps only feelings of annoyance and/or inconvenience). In this scenario, it could be convincingly argued that the individual was being cyberstalked (in many states this would be the case).

---

[4] Bocij and McFarlane (2002b) define harassment as emotional distress.

Clearly this individual was being pursued online—their stalker was trying to bring harm to them, and assert control over them, but for whatever reasons they weren't afraid, perhaps because they possess a high level of computer competence and feel in control (Spitzberg, 2006). This example raises the question of whether a virtual environment is qualitatively different than a physical or "real life" environment – a question that has not been addressed empirically or otherwise by researchers studying fear of crime, stalking, or cyberstalking. However, two recent studies are informative in considering the nature and influences on online fear of crime. For instance, Higgins, Ricketts, and Vegh (2008) examined fear of online victimization among Facebook users, and concluded that fear was a function of perceived risk, which was in turn associated with low self-control on the part of the Internet user. In another recent study, Henson (2011) explored fear of cyberstalking victimization among college students, concluding that at least 50% of study participants were afraid that their online information would be used to cyberstalk them. However, their intensity of fear and perceived risk of victimization were relatively low. This suggests that correlates of fear may differ across online and offline contexts.

Unfortunately, these two studies do not conclusively address the degree to which either fear or perceived risk are generated in online environments. Indeed, Henson's (2011) work revealed gender and relationship status as determinants of fear of online victimization, suggesting that feelings of fear and the intensity of fear are dynamic concepts that differ from individual to individual. Since research exploring the nature of fear of online crime is still developing and many questions related to online fear remain unanswered, fear is not treated as a criterion for cyberstalking victimization in the current study. This is not to say that cyberstalking does not illicit fear in victims; to the contrary, Reno (1999) suggests that cyberstalking can be just as frightening as being physically watched and followed. When the cyberstalking victimization field develops further, and when more is known about fear in online environments, this definition may need to be revisited.

Distinction between Stalking and Cyberstalking
Another point of disagreement among researchers is whether cyberstalking is essentially the same as or an extension of physically proximal stalking, save differences in tactics or techniques (Bocij, 2006; Bocij & McFarlane, 2003b; Henson, 2010). This is one of Bocij and McFarlane's (2003b) *Seven Fallacies about Cyberstalking*. These authors point out that cyberstalking must be different than traditional forms of stalking primarily for three reasons. First, it is different because governments, the media, and the press recognize it as distinct. For example, Attorney General Reno's report recognizes it as legally distinct, and some states have cyberstalking statutes apart from their stalking statutes. Second, some stalkers may never engage in pursuit behaviors outside of cyberspace, therefore it cannot be merely an extension of physically proximal stalking if none has occurred. Third, new technologies will always lead to new types of crime (e.g., before computers, there were no computer viruses) (Bocij & McFarlane, 2003b). The authors' second point is perhaps the most compelling. Clearly, if no physically proximal stalking occurs, but online stalking does, cyberstalking must be a separate phenomenon—one characterized by repeated *online* or *electronic* pursuit behaviors. Stalking includes a physical proximity component, which distinguishes it from cyberstalking. However, this still leaves the question of perpetrators who utilize a variety of techniques to pursue their victims, including both physically-based pursuit and online or electronic pursuit. Bocij (2003) suggests that the two types of stalking are qualitatively different. For example, according to Bocij, cyberstalking victims are less likely to know their stalkers than victims of physically proximal stalking. Similarly, cyberstalking purportedly takes place over a shorter period of time than stalking (Bocij, 2003).

Much like the issue of fear and cyberstalking, the crossover between physically proximal and online stalking has not been adequately addressed empirically. There has not been enough research for distinctions between stalking and cyberstalking to be made, although Sheridan and Grant (2007) argue that stalking and cyberstalking are not fundamentally different. Based on their analysis, these authors reported that along many dimensions stalking and cyberstalking incidents were comparable in terms of: the stalking process, the effect on victims, effects on third parties, victim responses, and stalker gender, among others. The position taken here is that at the very least cyberstalking *may* be distinctly different than physically proximal stalking, and this study is focused solely on electronic and online experiences which comprise cyberstalking victimization.

The Social Construction of Cyberstalking as a Problem
Among the general population, cyberstalking has been recognized as an important issue. In 1999, Attorney General Janet Reno released a report on cyberstalking that represents among the most comprehensive treatments of the subject to date. This report was the result of a concern on the part of Vice President Al Gore that cyberstalking was an emerging problem that needed to be addressed. In fact, the Vice President remarked that, "Make no mistake: this kind of harassment can be as frightening and as real as being followed and watched in your neighborhood or in your home" (Reno, 1999: 1). Accordingly, the Vice President asked the Attorney General to explore the extent of the problem, current practices for addressing the problem, the state of legislation related to cyberstalking, and to provide policy recommendations for meeting the new challenges created by cyberstalking. Ten years after that report was released, it is striking how little progress has been made toward understanding cyberstalking. Attorney General Reno recognized that the extent of cyber-stalking is unknown and that its frequency of occurrence is difficult to quantify, but argued that all indications are that it is a growing problem.

As an exercise in estimating the extent of cyberstalking, Reno pointed out that (at the time) there were 80 million adults and 10 million children in the United States with access to the Internet. Based on the finding in the National Violence Against Women Survey (NVAWS) that one percent of women and 0.4 percent of men had been stalked in the previous 12 months, Reno extrapolated that there could be tens or hundreds of thousands of cyberstalking victims every year[5].

---

[5] Reno acknowledged that these figures are purely speculative, but they do give some indication of the possible widespread nature of the problem as well as its potential magnitude.

Although no national statistics from law enforcement on cyberstalking were available at the time Reno's report was written, she did cite anecdotal evidence from law enforcement across the country suggesting that the number of cases of cyberstalking was growing to document the existence of the problem. Since that time, it is evident that based on small scale studies of cyberstalking and a few national estimates (which will be reviewed in the following section), as well as reports to law enforcement, and the recognition of this type of victimization among state and federal legislators that cyberstalking is a reality that many have faced.

While acknowledging that online harassment and related behaviors are undoubtedly distressing for victims, Ellison (1999) contends that much of the discourse on cyberstalking and online harassment has been fueled by the media, and may amount to nothing more than a moral panic (also Ellison & Akdeniz, 1998). Wykes (2007) argues that stalking and cyberstalking are essentially culturally constructed rehashes of the already existing crime of harassment, brought into the spotlight by celebrity victims of physically proximal stalking. Koch (n.d.) is quite blunt in his criticism of the cyberstalking "hysteria," going so far as to say the following:

> "There are problems on the Internet—some real, others minuscule, many imaginary. There are criminal financial dealings on the Net, child porn and child molesters, dope dealers and terrorists. It's like life—real and, at times, grim, ugly and desperate. But when it comes to cyberstalking, there's little justification for the hysteria."

As evidence that cyberstalking is merely a media hype, Koch suggests that the Fisher et al. (2002) study was the sole justification in the Reno (1999) report that cyberstalking exists. This is simply not the case, of course, as the Reno report also references the NVAWS[6], specific cases of cyberstalking victimization, reports of incidents from law enforcement throughout the nation, and information from Internet service providers regarding complaints of such behaviors.

---

[6] The NVAWS did not measure cyberstalking; however, Reno used numbers from the NVAWS to estimate the potential for cyberstalking in the United States.

This suggestion that cyberstalking is only a problem for a small portion of Internet users or doesn't exist in the first place is a minority opinion among commentators and researchers on the subject. Bocij and McFarlane (2002a), Jaishankar and Sankary (2005), and Pittaro (2008) rebuff detractors by arguing that current estimates indicate that thousands of cyberstalking incidents occur each year, and that victims suffer significant harm (e.g., psychological, financial) as a result of their victimization. Bocij and McFarlane (2003a) have suggested that the extent of the problem may have been overestimated in the media and various cyberstalking resource websites (e.g., CyberAngels, WHOA), but that at the very least there are likely 30,000 incidents each year in the United States alone[7]. Regardless, subsequent studies (Alexy, Burgess, Baker, & Smoyak, 2005; Baum et al., 2009; Bocij, 2003; D'Ovidio & Doyle, 2003; Finn, 2004; Fisher et al., 2002; Holt & Bossler, 2009; Jerin & Dolinsky, 2001; Reyns, Henson, & Fisher, 2011, 2012; Sheridan & Grant, 2007; Spitzberg & Hoobler, 2002) have revealed that cyberstalking happens, it is potentially widespread, it is serious, and it has real consequences for victims. The extent of cyberstalking victimization will be discussed following a review of the methodological challenges that affect cyberstalking estimates.

EXTENT OF CYBERSTALKING VICTIMIZATION

Before discussing the estimates of cyberstalking victimization from past studies, it should first be recognized that such estimates were at

---

[7] While Bocij and McFarlane (2003a) argue that there are at least 30,000 incidents each year in the United States based on information available from victim resource websites such as CyberAngels and Working to Halt Online Abuse (WHOA), the authors do not acknowledge the possibility that many of the incidents may be repeat victimizations of the same individuals. If this is the case, then reporting the number of incidents may be somewhat misleading. Unfortunately, the statistics that are available from these resources do not address the repeat nature of this crime, nor do they disclose whether they have taken repeat victimization into account when compiling their statistics.

times generated under less than ideal methodological circumstances, and hence must be approached with proper caution. Nevertheless, these existing estimates provide some idea of the extent of cyberstalking victimization. Methodological issues in estimating cyberstalking victimization will be discussed below, followed by estimates of stalking and cyberstalking victimization.

Methodological Issues in Estimating Cyberstalking Victimization

The lack of methodological consistency across studies of cyberstalking (e.g., methodologies, definition of cyberstalking used) makes comparisons difficult. Issues such as a lack of statistical analyses, a reliance on convenience samples, small sample sizes, and measuring cyberstalking through self-identification are among the limitations of previous work. Therefore, one of the primary goals of the current study is to improve upon many of the methodological deficiencies present in previous works examining cyberstalking victimization. A few methodological patterns across studies of cyberstalking warrant note.

Sampling Design Issues

With the exception of the Baum et al. (2009) report conducted by the Bureau of Justice Statistics as a supplement to the National Crime Victimization Survey[8], and the Fisher et al. (2002) study, all of the previous studies of cyberstalking victimization have relied on nonprobability samples. This is a potentially serious problem because nonprobability samples cannot be considered representative of any larger unobserved populations (an assumption that can be made of probability samples), and as a consequence the generalizability of the results are compromised as a result of sampling bias. Most prior studies that estimated the extent of cyberstalking victimization potentially suffer from sampling bias, and the estimates of cyberstalking derived from these studies must be considered in light of this limitation.

Sample size is another methodological issue of concern with respect to previous studies of cyberstalking victimization. Sample sizes from past works range from 154 to 4,446. Small sample sizes can limit the generalizability of results because there is less of a chance that the

---

[8] Other scholars have also begun to analyze this data, which provides a valuable resource in understanding the nature of cyberstalking victimization (e.g., Englebrecht & Reyns, 2011; Reyns & Englebrecht, 2010).

sample is representative of the larger population from which it was drawn. Usually, larger sample sizes are considered to be more representative of the population and yield more precise estimates of observations in the population.

Study Populations
The populations under study in previous works are quite diverse, ranging from female customers of online dating websites to the entire adult population of the United States. This makes comparisons across studies difficult, as theory would suggest different groups have differing levels of risk. However, about half of the studies have examined the cyberstalking victimization of college students, a focus which makes both theoretical and practical sense and allows for some comparison possibilities. The six college student-centered studies of cyberstalking victimization include: Fisher et al. (2002)[9], Spitzberg and Hoobler (2002), Finn (2004), Alexy et al. (2005), Holt and Bossler (2009), and Kraft and Wang (2010).

Defining and Operationalizing Cyberstalking as a Dependent Variable
While all of the studies of relevance to the current discussion are in some way measuring cyberstalking victimization (or some aspect of cyberstalking), none do so in precisely the same way (i.e., victimization is not measured in the same way across studies). For instance, Spitzberg and Hoobler (2002) have 24 questionnaire items to measure various elements of cyberstalking, while Baum et al. (2009) have a single-item measure of behaviors which caused the survey respondent to feel fear. The studies of cyberstalking that have been undertaken to date have mostly examined either the repeated contact or harassment elements of cyberstalking. Few researchers have taken a multidimensional (i.e., use of multi-item measures of cyberstalking) approach to the task. Nearly all have neglected identity fraud, threats of violence, and sexual harassment as aspects of the crime, with the sole exception of Bocij (2003).

---

[9] Fisher et al. (2002) focused exclusively on college women.

Bocij's (2003) study offered a multi-faceted approach (i.e., considering a various dimensions of cyberstalking), but each of the components of cyberstalking were estimated separately. Identity theft was measured, repeated harassment was measured, and so on, but a measure capturing all of these was not created. Spitzberg and Hoobler's (2002) study may come the closest to measuring all of the various behaviors that comprise cyberstalking, but this study suffers from a different methodological shortcoming—namely, a problematic definition of cyberstalking. Stalking and cyberstalking are *by definition* repeat victimizations (see Davis & Frieze, 2002; Fisher, 2001; Fisher et al., 2002). Spitzberg and Hoobler did not take this into account when they constructed their measures of cyberstalking victimization, or did so only implicitly. The authors report the percentage of their sample that had experienced a host of harassment behaviors *at least once*. To illustrate, one of their survey questions reads, "Has anyone ever undesirably and obsessively communicated with or pursued you through your computer or other electronic means by sending threatening written messages?" (Spitzberg & Hoobler, 2002: 83). Based on this question and 23 other questions asking about online behaviors and experiences, the authors constructed three composite measures of cyberstalking over the course of three pilot studies. As noted, this study suffers from a major definitional shortcoming—the repeat nature of cyberstalking was not caputured.

The issue of how cyberstalking is defined and operationalized is an important one because it most certainly affects measurement and estimates of the extent of victimization (as has also been shown to be the case with traditional stalking; see Fisher, 2001). This is a question of validity—specifically, face validity. Since repeated pursuit behaviors (i.e., behaviors that happened on two or more occasions) were not measured in Spitzberg and Hoobler's (2002) study, and the authors did not report to what extent respondents experienced more than one type of cyberstalking behavior, it is unclear whether this study actually documented the occurrence of cyberstalking.

Finn (2004) addressed the definitional limitation of the Spitzberg and Hoobler (2002) study by asking respondents if harassment behaviors were repeated (i.e., 1-2 times, 3-5 times, 5 or more times), rather than asking if respondents had ever experienced certain behaviors (e.g., one time only). However, Finn suggests that his study does not actually measure cyberstalking because his survey questionnaire did not ask whether respondents were fearful as a result of their experiences. He further notes the difficulty in comparing cyberstalking estimates across studies because of differences in the definition used across studies and a lack of conceptual clarity (Finn, 2004). However, Finn's study warrants discussion for two reasons, the first being conceptual and the second being definitional. First, according to many state statutes (see Appendix 1) Finn's dependent variable (online harassment) actually was a type of cyberstalking. Second, according to the definition of cyberstalking adopted for the present study, the behaviors he measured were behaviors that can be considered cyberstalking. Finn's (2004) study will be discussed further below.

Research Design
Finally, every estimate of cyberstalking victimization to date has been based on a study in which a cross-sectional design was used. In general, longitudinal designs are superior to cross-sectional designs in establishing causal relationships between independent and dependent variables. However, it is often difficult to obtain longitudinal data, especially longitudinal data on stalking. To date, no stalking or cyberstalking estimate has been generated utilizing a longitudinal design.

Estimates of Stalking Victimization
A growing body of stalking victimization research indicates that a large proportion of the general public has experienced stalking. Estimates on the extent of stalking victimization primarily come from three national-level studies in the United States, as well as several smaller-scale studies. The most recent of the national-level studies was conducted in 2006 as a Stalking Victimization Supplement (SVS) to the National Crime Victimization Survey (NCVS). According to the BJS report, 3.4 million individuals over 18 years old in the United States were reportedly victims of stalking in the previous 12 months (Baum et al., 2009). In comparison, the National Violence Against Women Survey (NVAWS), a second nationally representative survey of stalking in the United States, estimates that there were 1.4 million victims of stalking in the year preceding the survey (Tjaden & Thoennes, 1998). It is not

clear what this apparent growth in stalking victimization can be attributed to, but one plausible explanation is the proliferation of interpersonal communication technologies. These technologies have the potential to facilitate a number of types of electronic pursuit (i.e., cyberstalking). In other words, while speculative, one of the reasons for this growth may be an increase in cyberstalking victimization.

The third nationally representative survey of stalking victimization focused exclusively on college women. According to Fisher et al. (2002), 13.1% of the sample of female college students had been stalked at least once since the beginning of the academic year. A number of subsequent studies have confirmed the findings derived from these three national studies—namely, that a substantial portion of the population experiences physically proximal stalking (see Spitzberg & Cupach, 2007; Tjaden, 2009), but that the extent of cyberstalking is less understood.

Estimates of Cyberstalking Victimization
The study of cyberstalking victimization is in the very early stages—to date very few empirical examinations (e.g., Alexy et al., 2005; Bocij, 2003; Jerin & Dolinsky, 2001; Sheridan & Grant, 2007; Spitzberg & Hoobler, 2002) of this type of victimization have been undertaken. Aside from this limited body of cyberstalking studies, additional knowledge about cyberstalking victimization comes from larger studies of traditional stalking that have also measured online pursuit (e.g., Baum et al., 2009; Fisher et al., 2000, 2002). These works are methodologically sound; however, cyberstalking was not the primary focus of the respective studies, so their usefulness in explaining what factors put individuals at risk is rather limited. Other informative works have stopped short of explicitly discussing cyberstalking, instead focusing on its component behaviors such as online harassment only (Bossler et al., 2011; Finkelhor, Mitchell, & Wolak, 2000; Finn, 2004; Holt & Bossler, 2009; Marcum, Higgins, & Ricketts, 2010).

A review of the extant research literature yielded only eleven studies that have attempted to estimate the extent of cyberstalking victimization in any systematic way. Table 1.1 briefly summarizes these studies as well as those studies of physically proximal stalking which also measured cyberstalking (and have attempted to estimate its scope). Estimates of the extent of cyberstalking victimization vary widely across these studies. Indeed, even amongst those studies examining similar populations (i.e., college students), the victimization rate ranges between 3.7% and 31%.

Bocij's (2003) research was among the first attempts to estimate the prevalence of cyberstalking. This exploratory study was based on the analysis of responses from 169 individuals who participated in a web-based survey. The sample for this study was generated through snowball sampling techniques, a technique which poses serious external validity concerns. Despite these methodological limitations, the study gives us some indication of the scope of cyberstalking. The author reported that 21.9% of respondents could be classified as victims of cyberstalking when a conservative estimate[10] was employed (otherwise, the more liberal estimate[11] indicated that over 82% of respondents had been victimized).

The possible limitations of Spitzberg and Hoobler's (2002) study have already been discussed, but if we accept that the authors did indeed measure cyberstalking victimization then their results indicate that up to 31% of the sample had been cyberstalked at some point in their lives. As with the Bocij (2003) study, the Spitzberg and Hoobler (2002) study relies on a small convenience sample (235 undergraduate college students) and features questionable representativeness (both in terms of college students and college students at the particular institution from which the sample was drawn). The authors fully acknowledged the possible shortcomings of their methodological approach by stipulating that the study was exploratory.

---

[10] This estimate required that two or more incidents had taken place, that all incidents be perpetrated by the same person, that the incident caused the victim distress, and that the stalking behaviors be carried out through Internet communications technology.

[11] This estimate is based on respondents indicating that they had experienced at least one of any number of possible online behaviors (e.g., abusive emails, threats). A total of 17.9% of respondents indicated they had not experienced any such behaviors.

Table 1.1: Summary of Cyberstalking Victimization (CSV) Studies

Authors (year)	Operationalization of Dependent Variable	Estimate of Extent of CSV
Jerin and Dolinsky (2001)	7 items – e.g., threatening email, electronic identity theft	26.8%
Fisher et al. (2002)	Repeatedly emailed in a way that seemed obsessive or resulted in feelings of fear	24.7% (of those who were stalked)
Spitzberg and Hoobler (2002)	Being harassed or obsessively pursued through the computer or other electronic means – 24-item scale of cyberstalking behaviors	< 31%
Bocij (2003)	11 measures of online harassment through different tactics (e.g., threatening emails, computer viruses)	21.9% - 82%
D'Ovidio and Doyle (2003)	Aggravated harassment in which the offender used a computer or the Internet to commit the offense	42.8% (of cybercrimes)
Finn (2004)	Repeated messages meant to harass, threaten or insult via email or IM, including being sent pornography	10% (nonstrangers) 15% (strangers)
Alexy et al. (2005)	Not provided	3.7% (cyberstalking only) - 31.5% (in addition to stalking)
Sheridan and Grant (2007)	Incidents persisting for <4 weeks on <10 occasions that included unsolicited emails and harassment via the Internet	7.2%
Baum et al. (2009)	Conduct which causes respondent to feel fear via unsolicited or unwanted emails	26.1% (of those who were stalked)
Holt and Bossler (2009)	Dichotomous measure of online harassment (through chat client) in last 12 months	18.9%
Kraft and Wang (2010)	Repeated harassment through online communications that causes the victim to feel fear	9%

Finn (2004) examined a convenience sample comprised of 339 undergraduate students from the University of New Hampshire and utilized a survey to collect the data related to online harassment. Finn reported that approximately 10% of survey respondents had experienced some form of online harassment (e.g., getting repeated messages from a significant other that threatened, insulted, or harassed) committed by someone they knew (e.g., acquaintance, friend, spouse). Additionally, approximately 15% experienced these same sorts of behaviors committed by someone they did not know. The results further indicated that 3.5% of respondents had received repeated email messages from someone after asking them to stop, and 3% received repeated instant messenger (IM) messages after asking the offender to stop.

Jerin and Dolinsky (2001) examined the cybervictimization of women who used Internet dating services. Based on an online survey of randomly selected women[12] who used three particular online dating services, the authors were able to identify certain tactics that the cyberstalkers employed in the online victimization of women. Jerin and Dolinsky did not disclose how they defined cyberstalking, but up to 26.8% of their sample experienced one of seven behaviors that can potentially be labeled as cyberstalking (e.g., receiving threatening email, being the target of electronic identity theft). This study also offers information on the forms that cyberstalking takes. For instance, the authors reported that obscene emails were the most frequently occurring method of cyberstalking (N = 36), followed by online verbal abuse (N = 21), junk emails (N = 21), and threatening emails (N = 11) (Jerin & Dolinsky, 2001).

In a study of cyberstalking utilizing official data rather than self-report surveys (as every other study of cyberstalking has done), D'Ovidio and Doyle (2003) used data from the New York Police Department's Computer Investigation and Technology Unit (CITU) to

---

[12] The analysis was based on 134 cases, and the response rate for the survey was 10.75%.

examine information about victims and methods of cyberstalking. The data represented all closed cases of aggravated harassment between 1996 and 2000 in which computers or the Internet were involved. Of all cybercrimes investigated by CITU during that period, cyberstalking was the most prevalent (42.8% of cases[13]), and 40% of these cases were closed with an arrest.

Sheridan and Grant (2007) examined questionnaires completed by 1,051 self-defined stalking victims. These authors used conservative criteria before labeling an incident as either stalking or cyberstalking (i.e., as per Pathé et al., 2000), and stalking was considered to have taken place if the behaviors persisted for over four weeks and occurred on ten or more occasions) (Sheridan & Grant, 2007). Based on this conservative criteria, the authors reported that of those self-identified stalking victims 47.5% reported that at least some of the harassment occurred over the Internet; however, only 7.2% of the sample was determined to have been cyberstalked. Further, 4% of the total sample was judged to have been stalked purely online.

The authors of this study also provided information about cyberstalkers and the consequences of cyberstalking. For instance, cyberstalking victims were more likely to be stalked online by acquaintances or strangers than ex-partners, and police reportedly took victims who had only been stalked online more seriously than those who had been stalked both online and offline. Interestingly, those incidents involving crossover between cyberstalking and stalking[14] were reported to involve the most extreme and physically dangerous stalking behaviors. After comparing stalking and cyberstalking victimization

---

[13] Of cases that were closed, information about offenders revealed that most often offenders were male (80%), white (74%), and fairly young (average age of 24). Similar information about victims was also reported, which suggested that victims were most often female (52%), white (85%), and an average of 32 years old. Consistent with other research into the tactics used by cyberstalkers, email was the most frequently used method of communication for cyberstalkers (79%), followed by instant messengers (13%).

[14] For the purposes of statistical analyses, the authors divided their sample into four groups: purely online, cross-over, proximal with online, and purely offline. Of those in the cross-over group, the stalking started online and persisted for at least four weeks before making the crossover to the physical world.

incidents from their sample, the authors argued that the two are "indistinguishable" in terms of the stalking process and the effects on victims (Sheridan & Grant, 2007: 636). The authors admitted to the problems associated with a self-defining sample, and a lack of generalizability, but nevertheless claim that this study had demonstrated that cyberstalking and stalking are not fundamentally different crimes.

Kraft and Wang (2010) estimated the extent of both cyberstalking and cyberbullying among a sample of 471 college students from a single public liberal arts college. In this study, respondents were given a definition of cyberstalking and cyberbullying along with examples, and asked if they had ever experienced these behaviors. Cyberstalking was defined as "…repeated harassment through the Internet, email, or other electronic communication that causes the victim to fear for their safety. Technology is used to stalk the victim with the intention of annoying, alarming, or threatening the victim" (Kraft & Wang, 2010: 80). Based on this definition, Kraft and Wang estimated that 9% of their sample had been victims of cyberstalking. As a side note, they also estimated that 10% had been cyberbullied.

Additional information on cyberstalking tactics have been provided by Working to Halt Online Abuse (WHOA), an organization dedicated to fighting online harassment (WHOA, 2009). WHOA reported that it receives 50-75 incidents of cyberstalking each week from across the globe and from various sources (e.g., law enforcement, direct communications from victims). Beginning in 2000, WHOA started asking victims to fill out questionnaires related to their experiences with cyberstalking, which means that WHOA now has nine years of data available on cyberstalking victimization. Sample sizes across the years range from 196 incidents in 2004 to 443 incidents in 2005. Since the persons answering WHOA's questionnaires have already been identified as cyberstalking victims, the extent of victimization cannot be estimated based on this data. However, certain information about the cyberstalking incidents and victims can be gleaned from these reports. For instance, from their 2008 statistics, WHOA (2009) reported that for 36% of victims email was the tactic used by the offender to stalk the victim online. The next most frequent method of cyberstalking was through online message boards (e.g., forums, newsgroups) at 11.5%, followed by other methods (e.g., dating sites, gaming sites) at 11% (WHOA, 2009). According to WHOA's 2008 statistics, victims of cyberstalking are most often: female (71%), 18-30 years old (35%), white (74%), and of unknown marital status (34%) or single (31%). WHOA also collects and reports information on cyberstalking offenders, a topic that has received even less research attention than cyberstalking victimization. WHOA (2009) reported that cyberstalkers are mostly male (42%), and previously in a relationship (e.g., ex-spouse, online dating) with their victims (57%).

Empirical Estimates of Cyberstalking from Larger Studies of Offline Stalking

Further empirical information on cyberstalking has been provided by scholars studying offline stalking. For instance, Fisher et al. (2000, 2002) surveyed a nationally representative sample of college women as part of a broader study about sexual victimization against college women that included stalking victimization. Fisher et al.'s definition of stalking required that two or more pursuit behaviors by the offender had taken place, as well as a feeling of concern or fear for one's safety on the part of the victim. As previously noted, the authors reported that 13.1% of sample respondents had been stalked in the preceding seven months. Additionally, of those women who had experienced stalking victimization, 24.7% (N = 166) had received emails from the stalker in the course of the stalking incident.

In another nationally representative sample, Baum et al. (2009) reported results from the Supplemental Victimization Survey (SVS) to the National Crime Victimization Survey (NCVS) which estimated the extent of stalking in the United States. The NCVS is based on a nationally representative sample of residents of the United States age 18 and older, and asks respondents about their victimization experiences as well as those of the household members over the past 12 months. As in the case of the Fisher et al. (2000, 2002) studies, the SVS identified stalking as experiences involving certain behaviors on two or more occasions, and a feeling of fear for one's well-being, or fear for the safety of a family member as a result of these pursuit behaviors. While the SVS does not measure cyberstalking per se, it does provide information on tactics employed by stalkers similar to those of cyberstalkers. Specifically, one-in-four stalking victims (26.1%) also experienced some form of cyberstalking. The most frequent method of cyberstalking experienced by victims was email (82.5%), followed by instant messages (35.1%), blogs or bulletin boards (12.3%), and Internet sites about the victim (9.4%) (Baum et al., 2009).

Unfortunately, the email cyberstalking estimates are not directly comparable between the Fisher et al. (2000, 2002) studies and the SVS, for two reasons. First, the SVS separated out how many victims of stalking were also victims of cyberstalking. Second, the studies by Fisher and colleagues estimated all those who were stalked offline and reported how many of those victims were the recipient of emails as part of their stalking victimization. Taken together, the results derived from these two independent studies suggest that cyberstalking is indeed a potential problem, regardless of whether it is restricted to the virtual world of the Internet or part of a crossover between cyberstalking and stalking in physical proximity to the victim.

Alexy et al. (2005) examined both stalking and cyberstalking among a sample of college students from a state university (N = 100) and a private university (N = 656). Students who participated in this study were presented with two scenarios and asked to provide feedback on whether they considered incidents in the scenarios to be stalking and/or cyberstalking. In addition, participants completed a questionnaire pertaining to their experiences with cyberstalking and their Internet use in general. Of relevance is the finding reported by the authors indicating that 3.7% of the total sample had experienced cyberstalking. Of those who had been stalked, 31.5% experienced some form of cyberstalking in addition to their offline stalking experiences. The authors did not disclose how they defined either stalking or cyberstalking, nor did they indicate whether they used descriptive language tapping cyberstalking behaviors in their questionnaire to determine whether respondents were stalked/cyberstalked or if they allowed respondents to identify themselves as stalking/cyberstalking victims.

Based on the works reviewed above, it is clear that the actual extent of cyberstalking victimization is not currently known, but estimates range from 3.7% (Alexy et al., 2005) to 31% (Spitzberg & Hoobler, 2002) of participants in each respective study. These numbers suggest that cyberstalking may be more prevalent than traditional stalking.

With respect to traditional stalking, Mustaine and Tewksbury (1999) reported that in their sample, 10.5% of women indicated they had been a victim of stalking in the past six months. Fisher et al. (2000, 2002) surveyed college women, and based on their nationally representative sample they reported that 13.1% of their sample had been stalked in the past seven months. When Tjaden and Thoennes (1998) used a "relaxed" definition[15] of stalking in their estimation of incidence in the last year, they reported that 1% to 6% of women in their sample had been stalked.

Risk Factors for Stalking and Cyberstalking Victimization
While previous empirical examinations of cyberstalking victimization have provided some illumination as to the techniques employed by cyberstalkers, little is known about the factors which place individuals at risk for cyberstalking victimization. The current study is an attempt to fill this gap in the literature by examining the lifestyles and routine activities of victims of cyberstalking. There is, however, some work with respect to stalking victims that is informative in hypothesizing what places college students at risk of cyberstalking victimization. At a general level, it is consistently reported that females are at greater risk of stalking victimization than are males (see Fisher, 2001). This finding appears to be mirrored in the cyberstalking research (e.g., D'Ovidio & Doyle, 2003; Holt & Bossler, 2009). The exception is Alexy et al. (2005) who reported that males were more likely to be cyberstalked than females. Victims of offline stalking are most often 18 to 29 years old, and in a majority of cases perpetrators and victims know each other (Fisher et al., 2002; Tjaden & Thoennes, 1998). Interestingly, in comparison to other race groups, Native Americans and Alaska Natives appear to be at greater risk of stalking victimization, a finding that has not as yet been adequately explained (Fisher et al., 2002; Tjaden & Thoennes, 1998). This does not appear to be the case with cyberstalking. The information that is available indicates that whites

---

[15] This estimate was contingent on how the authors defined stalking. The "relaxed" definition was based on respondents indicating that they were "a little" or "somewhat" frightened, whereas the more conservative definition determined stalking had taken place if respondents indicated they were "very frightened" or in "fear of bodily harm." The more conservative estimate indicated that prevalence for the preceding 12 months was 1.0%.

are overwhelmingly more likely to be cyberstalked than other race groups (e.g., D'Ovidio & Doyle, 2003).

Among college students specifically, demographic characteristics do not consistently separate stalking victims from nonvictims (Fisher & Stewart, 2007). This may be due to the fact that college students do not vary substantially with respect to demographic characteristics. For instance, college students are generally around the same age and have usually never been married. Fisher and colleagues' (2002) analysis of female college students indicated that those students who are victimized are more likely to come from affluent family backgrounds and to be undergraduates rather than graduate students. There are no comparable demographic data with respect to victims of cyberstalking.

Beyond demographic explanations of stalking, the extant research suggests that lifestyles and routine activities of college students are significant predictors of stalking. The studies reported by Mustaine and Tewksbury (1999) and Fisher et al. (2002) have been integral in providing support for this perspective. Mustaine and Tewksbury's examination of a sample of 861 college women revealed that victims of stalking were more likely than nonvictims to engage in lifestyles in which they were exposed to potential offenders (i.e., frequently going to the mall). Besides the variable measuring going to the mall, other relevant predictors of stalking included living off campus, being employed, and engaging in drinking and drug use behaviors, all of which are theoretically consistent with a lifestyle-routine activities perspective. Fisher et al.'s (2002) results are comparable to those of Mustaine and Tewksbury (1999). For instance, a propensity to be at places with alcohol, living alone, dating, and prior victimization were all significant predictors of stalking victimization for females. To date, only Holt and Bossler (2009, 2010) have examined cyberstalking from a lifestyle-routine activities perspective, but their work has focused exclusively on the harassment aspect of cyberstalking victimization. Holt and Bossler (2009) reported that individuals who use chat rooms and engage in computer-related deviance are more likely to be cyberstalked. There is clearly a need for more work examining cyberstalking from a lifestyle-routine activities perspective; the current study will address this gap in the cyberstalking literature directly.

Cyberstalking Summary—Current State of Knowledge

The impression one gets after examining the extant literature on cyberstalking is that there are more questions than answers. Previous works have made a convincing argument that cyberstalking is a specific type of victimization that warrants attention, but to date there have been only a handful of studies designed to estimate its scope, and even less that identify risk factors for victimization. Researchers' understanding of the topic is further hindered by relatively weak study designs, definitional inconsistencies, and the examination of convenience samples. Further, cyberstalking is a challenging topic to study because of the difficulty in obtaining sampling frames and representative samples of at-risk populations. In addition, for the most part previous work has not advanced beyond demographic explanations and descriptive analyses of victimization (e.g., females are more likely to be victimized). A lifestyle-routine activities approach to the study of cyberstalking will be a fruitful way to identify correlates of risk for cyberstalking victimization. Victims' online lifestyles and routine activities may place them at greater risk of online victimization. For instance, perhaps the amount of time one spends online operates to expose Internet users to more "risk" of online victimization. These sorts of issues will be addressed following a discussion of the lifestyle-exposure and routine activities perspectives.

CHAPTER 2
Lifestyle-Routine Activities Theory

THEORETICAL FRAMEWORK

Lifestyle-exposure theory and routine activity theory were introduced fairly recently to criminologists and victimologists, but have since enjoyed extensive empirical testing, refinement, and empirical support (e.g., Cohen, Felson, & Land, 1980; Cohen, Kluegel, & Land, 1981; Cook, 1986; Felson, 1995; Fisher, Daigle, & Cullen, 2010b; Fisher, Sloan, Cullen, & Lu, 1998; Henson, Wilcox, Reyns, & Cullen, 2010; Lynch, 1987; Messner & Blau, 1987; Miethe & McDowall, 1993; Miethe & Meier, 1990, 1994; Miethe, Stafford, & Long, 1987; Mustaine & Tewksbury, 1998, 1999, 2002; Reyns, 2011; Reyns et al., 2011; Sampson & Lauritsen, 1990; Schreck & Fisher, 2004; Schreck, Wright, & Miller 2002; Wilcox Rountree, Land, & Miethe, 1994). The overall lifestyle-routine activities perspective will be discussed in light of the fact that these theories are often combined or treated as one approach because of their common theoretical assumptions. Originally, these theories were written to account for direct-contact, predatory crimes, such as robbery and burglary; the current study is an attempt to adapt the perspective for application beyond crimes in which the offender and the victim (or the victim's property) intersect at the same time and in the same place. The rationale for adapting the perspective for explaining crimes that occur in cyberspace is presented in Chapter 3.

LIFESTYLE-EXPOSURE THEORY AND ROUTINE ACTIVITIES THEORY

Lifestyle-exposure theory and routine activities theory are both considered "opportunity" theories. This means that they both attribute crime to criminal opportunities that exist as part of everyday life (Cohen et al., 1981; Felson, 2002; Felson & Clarke, 1998; Wilcox et al., 2003). At the very least, criminal opportunity is considered a necessary condition for a crime to take place. Simply put, without a criminal opportunity there will be no crime. Lifestyle-exposure theory and routine activities theory both focus on the circumstances under which such opportunities are created, with only subtle differences differentiating the two. For one, the lifestyle-exposure perspective focuses on individual-level risk factors for victimization, while routine activities theory was originally conceived as a macro-level explanation for fluctuations in crime rates (Felson, 2008). Lifestyle-exposure theory purports that certain lifestyles expose individuals to risk of victimization (e.g., exposure to an offender), thus creating an opportunity for a crime to occur (Hindelang et al., 1978). Cohen and Felson (1979) considered criminal opportunity in terms of its component parts. That is, the authors maintained that three elements are required for a crime to occur: a suitable target, a motivated offender, and an absence of capable guardianship. These two theoretical perspectives will be discussed in detail separately below, followed by a review of the empirical support for the overall perspective, especially with regard to its application to the victimization of college students. Following this discussion, there will be an overview of theoretical refinements to the theories, including the influence of participation in deviant or criminal lifestyles, and the victim's degree of self-control on their victimization.

Lifestyle-Exposure Theory
Lifestyle-exposure theory, also referred to as lifestyle theory or lifestyle-opportunity theory, was introduced by Hindelang et al. (1978) in their book, *Victims of Personal Crime: An Empirical Foundation for a Theory of Personal Victimization*. The book included an analysis of the 1972-1974 National Crime Survey (NCS), which the authors used to study victimization patterns among a representative sample of residents living in the United States. Among the patterns of victimization uncovered by Hindelang et al. (1978) was that individuals possessing certain demographic characteristics were disproportionately victimized. For example, the NCS results showed that males were generally more often victims than females. Based on their analysis of the NCS data, the authors theorized that the patterns of victimization they observed across demographic groups (e.g., sex, age, race) were the result of differences in lifestyles across the demographic groups in question. For instance, sex is an often-mentioned demographic characteristic that is

associated with differences in lifestyle (e.g., men and women engage in different lifestyles). As an example, if females participate in more home-based lifestyles, they are exposed to fewer risky situations posed by strangers[16]. As a consequence of their lesser exposure to risk, it is hypothesized that females would be less likely to be victimized (at least by strangers) than males. If there are indeed differences in lifestyle as a function of sex that are influenced by role expectations, structural constraints, and adaptations, then theoretically these differences may expose males and females to differing degrees of risk of victimization.

Lifestyle, and therefore exposure, is also expected to vary based on race and age of the victim. Regarding age, for instance, it would not be controversial to suggest that people of different ages participate in different kinds of lifestyles. These lifestyle differences therefore expose individuals of different ages to varying levels of risk of victimization. For example, it has been consistently reported that younger people are more likely to be victimized than older people (e.g., Hindelang et al., 1978). According to lifestyle-exposure theory, the explanation for younger people experiencing higher rates of victimization would be that younger people participate in lifestyles that expose them to greater risks for victimization (e.g., staying out later, frequenting bars more often, associating with other young people). This exposure to risk is one of the key components of lifestyle-exposure theory.

An important consideration in lifestyle-exposure theory is what influences these differences in lifestyle. According to Hindelang et al. (1978), individual characteristics (i.e., age, sex, race, income, marital status, education, occupation) bring with them certain role expectations and structural constraints (i.e., economic, familial, educational, legal) which dictate how a person must adapt if they are to function in socially and legally acceptable ways. Role expectations are the first antecedents to lifestyle and are defined by the authors as, "...cultural norms that are associated with achieved and ascribed statuses of individuals and that define preferred and anticipated behaviors," (Hindelang et al.,

---

[16] Home-based lifestyles may expose females to greater risk for certain types of victimization such as domestic violence, incest, and child abuse.

1978: 242). In other words, it is hypothesized that people with certain characteristics and combinations of characteristics are expected to behave in certain ways, and these role expectations to some degree impose certain lifestyles upon individuals possessing that role. For example, marital status is an often-mentioned determinant of lifestyle in that married people are expected to be spend time with their spouse, often at home, and eventually raise a family—all activities that theoretically are not risky or likely to facilitate victimization (Cohen & Felson, 1979). This is in contrast to a young single male who would most likely spend his time with friends, going on dates, and in essence, staying out late and leading a lifestyle conducive to victimization.

The second antecedent to lifestyle posited by the authors is the structural constraints that are imposed by the larger social structure. The authors define these as, "…limitations on behavioral options that result from the particular arrangements existing within various institutional orders, such as economic, familial, educational, and legal orders," (Hindelang et al., 1978: 242). In other words, the larger social structure imposes limits on our behavior, be it in the form of laws governing our behavior or personal economic considerations limiting where we can live and in what activities we can participate (Hindelang et al., 1978).

Obviously, individuals possessing the same constellation of demographic characteristics do not necessarily follow identical lifestyles, which is why the lifestyle-exposure model accommodates the role of individual decision-making in determining lifestyle. The authors stipulated that these guides or limits on behavior (i.e., role expectations, structural constraints) as a result of demographic characteristics were further refined by individual adaptations to them. These adaptations can be either individual or group-level (i.e., subcultural) responses to role expectations and structural constraints. The inclusion of *adaptations* in the lifestyle-exposure theoretical model allows for individual skills, personality, beliefs and attitudes to be taken into account in ultimately determining the sort of lifestyle in which a person will engage. According to the authors, "Individuals adapt to structural constraints and role expectations in ways that result in regularities in behavioral patterns. What is important is that these include such routine activities as working outside the home, going to school, or maintaining a household, as well as typical leisure time pursuits. These daily routines constitute *lifestyle* as we use the term here," (Hindelang et al., 1978: 244).

Hindelang et al. (1978) hypothesized that participation in certain peer groups (associations), as determined by one's lifestyle, also exposes individuals to opportunities for personal victimization. The *principle of homogamy* stipulates that individuals possessing certain charac-characteristics are likely to associate with others possessing those same characteristics (e.g., teenage girls associate more with other teenage girls). It follows that if certain characteristics are associated with offending (e.g., being young and male), those who share those characteristics and associate with those potential offenders are more likely to be victimized themselves (i.e., they are exposed to more opportunities for personal victimization). For instance, young people (a high-risk group and high-offending group) who spend time with other young people are therefore exposed to greater opportunities for victimization as a function of the people with whom they spend time. In sum, individuals develop a lifestyle which conforms to the limits placed upon them by their role and the larger society, and it is the activities which comprise this lifestyle that determine one's degree of exposure to victimogenic situations and opportunities. Figure 2.1 illustrates the full lifestyle-exposure theoretical model, as outlined by Hindelang and colleagues. The dashed lines around the demographic characteristics indicate that the variables are not part of the causal order of the theoretical model; however, they still need to be considered in light of their potential influence on victimization.

Routine Activities Theory
Routine activities theory was originally devised by Cohen and Felson (1979) to explain upward changes in aggregate predatory crime rates in the United States following World War II. The authors examined data from 1947-1974 from a variety of sources (e.g., Current Population Survey) to test their hypothesis that the rising crime rates during those years could be attributed to changes in social activities at the societal level in the United States. These changes in societal routine activities included more women entering the labor force and attending college, leaving the home unoccupied and unguarded during the day. The change from home-based activities not only exposed these individuals

to more opportunities for personal victimization, it also provided opportunities for the now-unguarded homes to be targeted. However, being outside the home, or leaving one's property unguarded are not sufficient conditions to facilitate victimization. The authors stipulated that there are three essential elements to every criminal opportunity: *a motivated offender*, *a suitable target*, and *an absence of capable guardianship*. Eck (2003) has termed this triad the "crime triangle," which is pictured in Figure 2.2.

The *motivated offender* element is comparable to the earlier *exposure* concept introduced by Hindelang et al. (1978), both of which in some way are related to the notion of *proximity* (as in physical proximity to motivated offenders), a concept that has since appeared in studies utilizing the lifestyle-routine activities perspective (e.g., Cohen et al., 1981). The *suitable target* element of the theory has been conceived of in various ways to include aspects of *target attractiveness* (e.g., Cohen et al., 1981), as well as *target congruence*[17], which is characterized by *target vulnerability*, *target gratifiability*, and *target antagonism* (Finkelhor & Asdigian, 1996). Cohen and Felson (1979) also described products presenting attractive targets as possessing the characteristics of VIVA, or having Value, Inertia, Visibility, and Access. Clarke (1999) expanded the VIVA concept with a different acronym. According to Clarke, CRAVED items are attractive targets or "hot products" because they are Concealable, Removable, Available, Valuable, Enjoyable, and Disposable. In terms of cyberstalking, information about a potential victim (e.g., contact information, gender, passwords) may be a commodity items or commodities. The third side of the triangle, *absence of capable guardianship*, involves the presence of anyone (e.g., pedestrians, police) or anything (e.g., cameras, dogs) capable of preventing crime. It is hypothesized that all else being equal, more protected targets are less likely to be chosen as targets by offenders.

---

[17] The concept of target congruence was introduced in the context of the victimization of minors; however, the idea has applicability to other potential targets for victimization beyond children and minors.

Figure 2.1: The Lifestyle-Exposure Theoretical Model of Personal Victimization

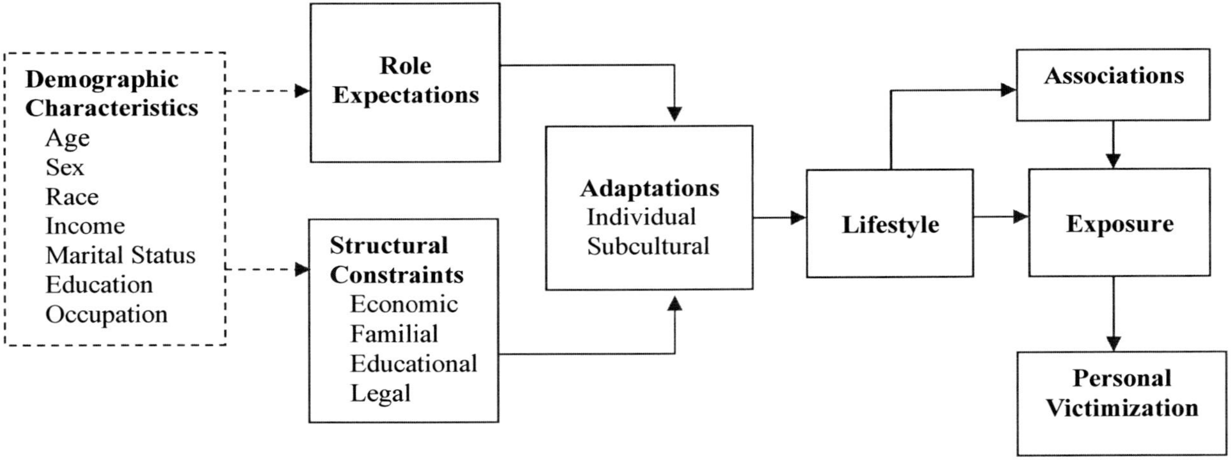

Source: Hindelang et al. (1978)

Figure 2.2: The Crime Triangle

```
        /\
       /  \
      /Mot.\ Suit.
     /Offen.\ Target
    /_____\
   Lack of Guardianship
```

Source: Adapted from Eck (2003).

According to Cohen and Felson (1979), the lack of one or more of these elements is sufficient to prevent crimes from occurring; however, little research has been focused upon which of these conditions is the most important, if any, or which factor makes the most difference with respect to criminal decision-making. The visual presentation of the crime triangle in Figure 2.2 may imply that each of the three components of the theory (i.e., motivated offender, suitable target, lack of guardianship) make an equal contribution to the creation of criminal opportunities. However, this may not be the case. Wilcox et al. (2003) have addressed this issue with their *dynamic view of criminal opportunity*, explaining several scenarios in which the amount of convergence in time and space of these concepts affects criminal opportunities, as well as the supply of motivated offenders, suitable targets, and environments lacking guardianship. For example, one scenario involves a context in which the supply of motivated offenders is low, the supply of suitable targets is high, and the availability of capable guardianship is high. In this scenario, we would expect relatively little criminal activity because even though the supply of potential targets is high, there is a low demand for and high guardianship of suitable targets (Cook, 1986; Wilcox et al., 2003).

Routine activities theory does not attempt to explain why offenders participate in crime, but rather focuses on those circumstances brought on by patterns of routine activities (e.g., work, family, leisure, school) which create criminal opportunities. In this sense then, routine activities theory is essentially the same as its sister theory, lifestyle-exposure theory. The key difference between the theories when *Social Change and Crime Rate Trends: A Routine Activity Approach* was published in 1979 was that Hindelang, et al.'s lifestyle-exposure theory was an individual-level theory of victimization while Cohen and Felson's routine activity approach was an aggregate-level theory of crime. Soon after the first routine activities article was published, the theory was adapted for use at the micro-level (e.g., Cohen et al., 1981; Miethe & Meier, 1990; Miethe et al. 1987), essentially bridging the gap between lifestyle-exposure theory and routine activities theory. In fact, Maxfield (1987) has written about the strong link between the two theories based on the similarities in their underlying concepts (i.e., lifestyles, routine activities), and Garofalo (1987) has argued that the two theories are very much alike.

Empirical Support for Lifestyle-Routine Activities Theory
Lifestyle-exposure and routine activities theories have implicitly been combined over the years as researchers have tested hypotheses about how lifestyles and routine activities expose individuals to risk of victimization. This largely unspoken fusion of the theories has resulted in a lifestyle-routine activities theory[18] (LRAT). The theories have been used to explain opportunities for different types for victimization (e.g., personal, property) across a wide range of environments (e.g., workplaces, places of leisure) and samples (e.g., adolescents, adults, college students) at different levels of analysis (i.e., micro, macro, meso). While not all tests of the perspective have corroborated the utility of the theories in explaining victimization (e.g., Massey, Krohn, & Bonati, 1989), the overall body of research has generally been supportive of the theories. Support for the lifestyle-routine activities perspective in explaining the likelihood of victimization of college students will be discussed later in the chapter.

---

[18] The terms lifestyle-routine activities theory, lifestyle theory, and routine activities theory will be used interchangeably in referring to the lifestyle-routine activities theory from this point forward.

THE APPLICATION OF LIFESTYLE-ROUTINE ACTIVITIES THEORY TO COLLEGE STUDENT VICTIMIZATION

Lifestyle-routine activities theory has been used successfully to explain the victimization of specific populations (e.g., adolescents, college students), and in line with Lynch's (1987) suggestion it has also been applied to victimization of individuals in different domains of life (e.g., places of work, college campuses). One of these populations, college students, is the focus of the current study. College students have been identified as being at risk for a variety of types of victimization, including stalking (for a review of college student victimization, see Fisher et al., 2010a). However, since routine activities theory has not been applied to the cyberstalking victimization of college students, it is necessary to consider those lifestyle-routine activities factors that have been identified as significant indicators of college student victimization generally.

A growing body of work has applied the lifestyle-routine activities perspective to college student victimization (e.g., Cass, 2007; Fisher et al., 1998; Holt & Bossler, 2009; Mustaine & Tewksbury, 1999; Schwartz & Pitts, 1995). These studies provide a starting point for determining which factors are important indicators of college student victimization generally, and which corresponding lifestyle-routine activities concepts are significantly related to victimization. Although the studies within this body of work focused upon a variety of different independent and dependent variables, clear patterns emerge in terms of risk factors for college student victimization. For instance, alcohol and drug use have been consistently identified as significant predictors of victimization (e.g., Cass, 2007). Related to this, participating in what may be considered risky activities or lifestyles (e.g., frequently partying, engaging in illegal activities) carry with them added likelihood of victimization (e.g., Fisher et al., 1998). For certain types of victimization (e.g., sexual assault), demographic characteristics may be indicators of target attractiveness, and these variables are generally found to increase one's likelihood of victimization. For instance, being female has been identified as a significant predictor of certain types of victimization (e.g., Mustaine & Tewksbury, 1998). Spending large sums of money on nonessential items, another measure of target attractiveness, has also been identified as a correlate of college student victimization (Fisher et al., 1998). Coming into contact with potential offenders (proximity) and being exposed or available for victimization (exposure) have also been reliable predictors of college student victimization. For instance, being friends with individuals who participate in deviant or illegal activities, a measure of proximity, has been identified as a precursor to a variety of types of victimization (e.g., Schwartz & Pitts, 1995). Likewise, frequently going out at night, a measure of exposure, has been consistently identified as a significant predictor of victimization (e.g., Mustaine & Tewksbury, 2002). Crime prevention measures and activities (guardianship) are theoretically expected to decrease one's likelihood of victimization; however, this has not always been the case. For instance, Fisher et al. (1998) reported that participating in crime prevention actions was significantly related to violent victimization, but asking someone to watch property instead of leaving it unattended was associated with a lower likelihood of theft victimization.

Considering only the few studies that have focused on the stalking and cyberstalking victimization of college students, the lifestyle-routine activities concepts of exposure, proximity, target attractiveness, and delinquent lifestyle have been identified as consistent indicators of victimization (Fisher et al., 2002; Holt & Bossler, 2009; Mustaine & Tewksbury, 1999). Each of these concepts has been reported to operate in the theoretically expected manner to increase college students' risk of stalking and cyberstalking victimization. However, the concept of guardianship has been less reliable in terms of operating in accord with theoretical expectations. Fisher et al. (2002) reported that, as expected, a lack of guardianship increased student stalking victimization. However, Mustaine and Tewksbury (1999) reported mixed results on the effects of guardianship, and Holt and Bossler (2009) found no statistically significant relationship between guardianship and victimization.

In sum, lifestyle-routine activities theory has demonstrated its usefulness in explaining the victimization of college students, including the stalking and cyberstalking victimization of college students, and most of the routine activity concepts (e.g., exposure, proximity) have been reported to behave in accord with theoretical predictions. More work is needed in the context of cyberstalking victimization to more fully explore the effects of the lifestyle-routine activities concepts.

THEORETICAL EXTENSIONS TO LIFESTYLE-ROUTINE ACTIVITIES THEORY

Through extensive empirical testing and theoretical refinements to lifestyle-routine activities theory, researchers have identified consistent correlates of victimization beyond the core elements of the theory discussed above (i.e., exposure, proximity, target attractiveness, and guardianship). Paramount among them are participation in deviant or criminal lifestyles and a propensity toward low self-control.

Deviant Lifestyles

One of the concepts central to lifestyle theory is that there are a variety of lifestyles in which individuals participate, and depending upon the routine activities associated with these lifestyles individuals are exposed to times and places with varying levels of risk for victimization (Hindelang et al., 1978). Not only do lifestyle patterns influence exposure to risks of victimization, but they also affect the frequency of interaction with those who are more or less likely to commit crimes (Garofalo, 1987). According to the principle of homogamy, "...an individual's chances of personal victimization are dependent upon the extent to which the individual shares demographic characteristics with offenders" (Hindelang et al., 1978: 257). It has also been suggested that there is a link between participation in delinquent and deviant lifestyles and risks of victimization (e.g., see Garofalo, 1987; Jensen & Brownfield, 1987). This relationship has been examined empirically, and research has confirmed the connection between deviant/offending lifestyles and victimization, although more recent research suggests that the relationship may be more complicated than previously thought (e.g., Gottfredson, 1984; Henson, et al., 2010; Jensen & Brownfield, 1987; Lauritsen & Laub, 2007; Lauritsen, Sampson, & Laub, 1991; Osgood, Wilson, O'Malley, Bachman, & Johnston, 1996; Sampson & Lauritsen, 1990; Schreck, Stewart, & Osgood, 2008). Further, the small body of research that has examined the effects of risky or deviant behaviors on online victimization suggests that engaging in these sorts of activities increases one's risks for online victimization (e.g., Bossler & Holt, 2009; Holt & Bossler, 2009; Wolak, Finkelhor, Mitchell, & Ybarra, 2008).

The Role of Self-Control

Gottfredson and Hirschi (1990) have argued that low self-control is the primary explanation for why individuals engage in not only criminal activities, but also experience other undesirable life events (e.g., failed relationships, unsuccessful careers). Once one's propensity toward self-control (e.g., low self-control) is established in early life, it is argued to remain fairly constant throughout the life course (Gottfredson & Hirschi, 1990). If a person has low self-control, they make decisions as if the consequences do not really matter and instead act to satisfy their immediate desires despite the likelihood of adverse long-term outcomes. This general theory of crime has received strong and consistent support since it was introduced by Gottfredson and Hirschi (1990). For example, Pratt and Cullen (2000) conducted a meta-analysis in which the results of 21 empirical studies were included, and concluded that low self-control was an important and robust predictor of crime and related behaviors.

Schreck (1999) suggested that this theory, which was originally conceived to explain offending behaviors, could be reformulated and used to account for victimization outcomes. In doing so, he helped to explain some of the overlap between victims and offenders. Schreck reported that low self-control could explain both property and personal victimization. That is, those with low self-control had greater odds of experiencing property and personal victimization. In addition, after taking the role of self-control into account statistically, demographic correlates of victimization (e.g., gender, income) exerted lesser influences on victimization outcomes.

Subsequent work by Schreck and others has solidified the role of self-control in explaining victimization. Schreck et al. (2002), for instance, utilized the lifestyle-routine activities perspective in conjunction with individual risk factors (e.g., low self-control, social ties) to explain violent victimization among adolescents. The authors reported that both individual traits and situational (i.e., opportunity) variables exhibited statistically significant effects in accounting for victimization. Expanding upon the idea that social ties, specifically ties to family and peers, can affect victimization risk through lifestyle-routine activities concepts (e.g., exposure, guardianship), Schreck and Fisher (2004) reported that adolescents with close ties to family were less likely to experience violent crime than adolescents lacking such ties. The authors also confirmed the role of delinquent peers in increasing one's chances of victimization through exposure to risky situations (Schreck & Fisher, 2004).

Schreck, Stewart, and Fisher (2006) further integrated self-control theory with lifestyle-routine activities theory, while also taking into account the effect of social ties, peer delinquency, and other known correlates of victimization. Once again, the authors reported that low-self-control was a robust predictor of victimization, even after considering the effects of past victimization, delinquency, delinquent peers, and social bonds (Schreck et al., 2006). Holtfreter, Reisig, and Pratt (2008) utilized routine activities theory and low self-control in an effort to account for a nonviolent type of victimization—fraud. Like previous work by Schreck and colleagues, the authors found support for routine activities and low self-control in explaining fraud victimization. These studies represent a sampling of the mounting body of work that highlights the importance of low self-control as an explanation for victimization (e.g., Fox, Gover, & Kaukinen, 2009; Piquero, MacDonald, Dobrin, Daigle, & Cullen, 2005; Stewart, Elifson, & Sterk, 2004).

The Role of Self-Control in Electronic/Online Environments
The body of research utilizing low self-control to explain victimization outcomes has largely focused on violent and property crime victimization, and suggests that overall this latent trait is useful in accounting for these types of victimization. However, to date no studies have examined cyberstalking victimization from a low self-control perspective. The question then becomes, why would someone with low self-control be more vulnerable to cyberstalking victimization? The answer is twofold—first, individuals with low self-control may be more likely to *make choices* that: (1) expose them to risk of cyberstalking victimization (e.g., spending more time online, visiting "riskier" websites); (2) bring them into online proximity with motivated offenders (e.g., granting strangers access to social network profiles or blogs); (3) lower their self-guardianship while online (e.g., these individuals may not guard their sensitive information as closely as someone with higher self-control); or, (4) present more attractive targets (e.g., posting photos of themselves in provocative poses). Second, lower self-control likely *affects the nature of one's electronic/online interactions*. For instance,

those with a propensity toward low self-control may be more abrasive and aggressive in their online interactions, perhaps annoying others during online communications (e.g., in chat rooms, instant message communications, text messages), antagonizing the potential offender into retaliation via threats, sexual advances, or other types of harassment. It becomes important therefore to consider how low self-control affects likelihood of cyberstalking victimization in conjunction with their online lifestyles and routine activities.

Summary—Refinements to Lifestyle-Routine Activities Theory

The identification of deviant and delinquent lifestyles as a correlate of victimization was a valuable discovery for victimologists. Mustaine and Tewksbury (1998) and others have argued that lifestyle-routine activities theory will benefit from research utilizing more specific and refined measures of lifestyles, and the identification of deviant lifestyles as a significant predictor of a variety of types of victimization certainly validates their argument. To illustrate, in a study of adolescent victimization, Henson et al. (2010) identified 11 distinct adolescent lifestyles and routine activities (e.g., family-oriented lifestyle, electronic lifestyle, work-centered lifestyle), including a delinquent lifestyle, which overwhelmed the other lifestyles as predictors of violent victimization. In addition, researchers have only recently begun to pursue the idea that there are electronic or online lifestyles as a distinct type of lifestyle that may influence victimization risk. Holt and Bossler (2009), for instance, have indicated that similar to traditional deviant lifestyles, deviant online activities (e.g., piracy) may be tied to online victimization (see also Bossler & Holt, 2010). Accordingly, the current study will consider the effects of online delinquency in predicting cyberstalking victimization.

As with the discovery of deviant lifestyles as a correlate of victimization, Schreck's (1999) suggestion that low self-control explains victimization has been an important addition to the routine activities literature. Schreck and colleagues have made a valuable contribution to the field of victimology by proposing that a criminological theory be extended for use in the study of victimization. To date, low self-control has not been considered in terms of cyberstalking victimization; however, it has been applied to cybercrime offending. For instance, Higgins (2005) examined the role of low self-control, delinquent peers, and attitudes toward software piracy and found that there was a link between low self-control and media piracy. In light of the link between low self-control and victimization, and low self-control and cybercrime, the current study will consider the effects of low self-control on cyberstalking victimization.

CHAPTER 3
The Theoretical Transition to Cyberspace

The lifestyle-routine activities perspective has not been applied to cybercrimes nearly to the degree that it has been to other, more traditional crimes; however, it is clear that this point warrants proper discussion. At its inception the theory was premised on the intersection in time and space of motivated offenders, suitable targets, and environments lacking guardianship. As the cybercrime victimization literature has grown over time, more studies applying the theory to these types of crimes have been published. However, most of these have assumed that this perspective, premised on an intersection in time and space, should apply to crimes in which time and place are immaterial without explaining why it should, a point that will be revisited in Chapter 6. The relevant literature will be presented and discussed below (e.g., Choi, 2008; Eck & Clarke, 2003; Holt & Bossler, 2009; Marcum, 2009; Marcum, Higgins, & Ricketts, 2010; Marcum, Ricketts, & Higgins, 2010; Newman & Clarke, 2003; Pratt, Holtfreter, & Reisig, 2010; Reyns, 2011; Yar, 2005), and arguments made for how a place-based theory can be adapted and applied to placeless crimes.

CYBERSPACE ENVIRONMENTS

Clarke (2004) has pointed out that globalization and new technologies have created considerable new opportunities for crime, and that the new environments in which these opportunities reside have substantial implications for criminology. However, there is considerable uncertainty over whether current criminological theories, including lifestyle-routine activities theory, are applicable to virtual environments (McQuade,

2006; Yar, 2005, 2006). The study of cybercrime has not yet fully answered the question of whether such crimes are inherently different than their terrestrial counterparts, making theorizing difficult (Grabosky, 2001). With respect to lifestyle-routine activities theory, Yar (2005) has argued that certain aspects of the theory (i.e., motivated offenders) can easily be adapted to virtual environments. He also, somewhat more reluctantly, accepts the possibility of envisioning suitable targets and capable guardianship in cyberspace, although he points out that it may be difficult to institute capable guardianship in virtual environments (Yar, 2005). The problem, according to Yar (2005), is that routine activities theory is premised on the spatial-temporal convergence of the three core concepts (i.e., motivated offenders, suitable targets, ineffective guardianship) and virtual environments are inherently timeless and do not exist in space, or in Yar's words are "spatio-temporally disorganized" (Yar, 2005: 424).

Network Problems

Eck and Clarke's (2003) work in fusing routine activity theory with problem-oriented policing helps shed some light on the issue of space and time with respect to routine activities theory in cyberspace. While not specifically speaking to the applicability of the theory to cyberspace, Eck and Clarke (2003) contend that the theory *can* be used to success in situations in which victims and offenders interact at some distance (e.g., mail bombing, harassing phone calls, telemarketing fraud). The authors explain that in the context of police problems, this is known as a *systems problem*. In a systems problem, the victim and offender converge not in space, but within a network (e.g., telephone and Internet systems, mail/package delivery). Further, in the context of online victimization, motivated offenders and targets do not necessarily have to converge online at the same time. Figure 2.3 illustrates the theoretical transition of the convergence of targets and offenders from places to networks.

Reyns (2010) has hypothesized that targets and offenders come together through a network, but the victimization incident may transpire many times within an online place. These online places can be chat rooms, social networks, auction sites, and other web domains (e.g., email clients). In other words, victims and offenders still intersect, but the "place" in which they intersect is an online place or web domain. Figure 2.4 further refines the crime triangle to accommodate cybercrimes.

The Theoretical Transition to Cyberspace 47

Figure 3.1: The Transition from Places to Networks

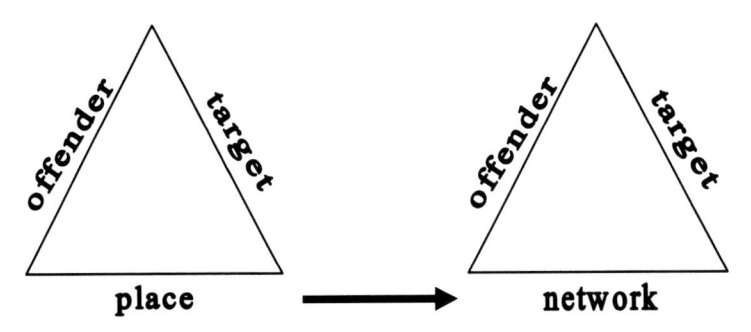

[Two triangles shown side by side with an arrow between them. Left triangle labeled "place" at the base, with "offender" and "target" on the left and right sides. Right triangle labeled "network" at the base, with "offender" and "target" on the left and right sides.]

Source: Eck and Clarke (2003).

The notion that websites can be places in which crimes take place has a number of implications for crime prevention theory. For instance, if websites can be considered online places, then it is reasonable to expect cybercrimes to concentrate at specific places online just as they do at physical locations such as bars, shopping malls, sports venues, or other busy places (e.g., Brantingham & Brantingham, 1995; Eck, Clarke, & Guerette, 2007; Sherman, Gartin, & Buerger, 1989; Spelman, 1995; Townsley, Homel, & Chaseling, 2000; Weisburd, Bushway, Lum, & Yang, 2004; Weisburd et al., 1992). With respect to cyberstalking, web domains are the places where victims and offenders converge, allowing the stalker access to the victim. In most cases, this web domain interaction facilitates the cyberstalking victimization by bringing together these two parties that otherwise would not have converged.

Figure 3.2: Routine Activities in an Online Domain

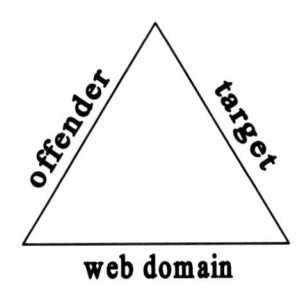

[Triangle labeled "web domain" at the base, with "offender" and "target" on the left and right sides.]

SCAREM

In a further modification of crime prevention theory for application to cyberspace environments, Newman and Clarke (2003) have argued that cybercrime environments by their very nature have criminogenic properties. Similar to Clarke's (1999) earlier acronym used to describe hot products (CRAVED), Newman and Clarke (2003) describe elements of information systems that are themselves conducive to crime using the acronym SCAREM. SCAREM stands for Stealth, Challenge, Anonymity, Reconnaissance, Escape, and Multiplicity. It is evident that many websites and online domains have the criminogenic qualities of SCAREM. For example, social networking websites provide not only fertile ground for cyberstalking to take place (e.g., public network pages provide viewers with complete anonymity), but also a wealth of potential victims (multiplicity). In this way, not only do web domains facilitate the convergence of victims and offenders within the network, but according to Newman and Clarke (2003), the nature of web domains encourages it through their criminogenic properties.

LIFESTYLE-ROUTINE ACTIVITIES IN CYBERSPACE

While scholars have debated the applicability of lifestyle-routine activities theory to cybercrime victimization, there have been few attempts to apply the theory to cybercrimes, and none have focused upon cyberstalking[19]. A review of academic databases (e.g., Academic Search Complete, Lexis Nexis Academic) using relevant keywords (e.g., routine activity, cybercrime) turned up a small number of empirical studies utilizing the theory to explain cybercrime victimization. These studies are divided into those examining college student populations and those based on other populations (e.g., adolescents, general populations).

College Student Studies
Although lifestyle-routine activities theory has been used by researchers to examine risk factors associated with college student victimiza-

---

[19] The exceptions being studies based on the same data as the current study (Henson, Reyns, & Fisher, 2011; Reyns, Burek, Henson, & Fisher, forthcoming; Reyns et al., 2011, 2012).

tion, including stalking, only seven[20] studies have utilized the perspective to explain the cybercrime victimization of college students, and none of these explores cyberstalking victimization (Bossler & Holt, 2009, 2010; Choi, 2008; Holt & Bossler, 2009; Marcum, 2009; Marcum et al. 2010a, 2010b). Each of these seven studies is discussed in detail below.

Choi (2008) used lifestyle-exposure theory and routine activities theory to explain computer crime victimization (i.e., computer virus infection) among a sample of 204 college students at a small liberal arts college in Pennsylvania. The author adapted the concept of lifestyle to online realms by asking students about their activities while online. Online lifestyles were broken down into three categories: vocational and leisure activities (scale composed of indicators such as frequency of sending emails), risky leisure activities (scale composed of indicators such as frequency of downloading materials while online), and risky vocational activities (scale with indicators such as frequency of opening email attachments). Of the three routine activity concepts, the author did not address motivated offenders or suitable targets, instead concentrating solely on the concept of guardianship. Guardianship was conceived of as *digital guardianship* and was measured using two sets of three-item scales (i.e., one scale tapping number of security programs, and one scale tapping duration of having security programs). The details related to Choi's (2008) operationalization of key concepts are important because this may have been the first attempt to operation-

---

[20] Seven studies excluding those based on the data utilized in the current study have been published to date. However, with the exception of Choi's (2008) research, there is a great deal of overlap between these studies. For example, Marcum's (2009) book was revised and presented as a journal article (Marcum et al., 2010a) with few if any differences in substantive content (see also Marcum et al., 2010b). Similarly, Bossler and Holt's research (2009, 2010) includes three articles based on the same data set, but examining different dependent variables (see also Holt & Bossler, 2009). Each of these studies are discussed on their own merits, recognizing that there is a good deal of overlap between those written by the same authors.

alize these concepts into a cyber-relevant form. The author reported that, consistent with expectations, those persons engaging in riskier online lifestyles were more likely to contract computer viruses, as were those who neglected their computer security. Additionally, those individuals with tighter online security (higher digital guardianship) were less likely to be victims of computer viruses.

Like Choi, Bossler and Holt (2009) examined the malware infection experienced by college students in the course of their online activities, and specifically whether the student lost data as a result of the malware infection. The authors concentrated primarily on the guardianship element of routine activities theory, in addition to measuring a number of specific online routines (e.g., playing video games, visiting chat rooms, downloading files), and participation in online deviance (i.e., pirating software, hacking). In estimating the effect of guardianship in preventing cybervictimization, the authors operationalized the concept into a "trifecta" of guardianship: personal guardianship (i.e., computer proficiency, protecting passwords), physical guardianship (e.g., using anti-virus software, hardware firewalls), and social guardianship (i.e., friends pirating media, friends pirating software). The results of this study indicate that guardianship does not protect individuals from losing data due to malware infections, as expected. To the contrary, social guardianship (i.e., deviant peers) increased the likelihood that students would be victimized. Further, the online deviant behaviors of students, particularly pirating media, increased their likelihood of losing data due to a malware infection. Although the authors argue that this study provides support for the application of routine activities theory to cyberspace environments, it seems to provide more support for the lifestyle-exposure elements of lifestyle-routine activities theory (i.e., deviance, deviant peers).

Holt and Bossler's (2009) study of online harassment was among the first to apply lifestyle-routine activities theory to a person-based type of cybervictimization. The authors used a self-report survey methodology to gather information from college students (N = 578) regarding their patterns of Internet use (e.g., skill level, shopping) and information about their experiences online (e.g., harassment). Like Choi's (2008) research, Holt and Bossler emphasized estimating the effects of online guardianship (e.g., use of anti-virus software, firewalls), and did not address the role of motivated offenders; they addressed target suitability only indirectly. Target suitability was measured with proxies, specifically gender and age. Exposure to risk was measured through the questions asking about computer usage. For instance, owning a computer, the amount of time spent online, use of Myspace, instant messengers, and chat rooms all indicate an added amount of exposure to risk that otherwise would not exist offline. The authors reported only mild support for lifestyle-routine activities theory in this context. Online routine activities did not exhibit statistically significant effects on harassment victimization, nor did general online exposure or guardianship. However, spending time participating in computer-related deviance (i.e., pirating media, viewing pornography, hacking) did increase one's odds of online victimization. Additionally, having friends involved in computer deviance increased the odds of harassment.

In a study that mirrored their 2009 research, Bossler and Holt (2010) examined cybervictimization with respect to five types of online behaviors: (1) unauthorized password access; (2) unauthorized access and alteration of computer information of files; (3) malware infection (e.g., computer viruses, worms); (4) electronic theft of credit card number; and, (5) online harassment. Bossler and Holt utilized the same data from previous studies, which was collected through a self-report survey from a purposive sample of college students at a southeastern university (N = 573). In addition to individual respondent characteristics, such as gender, race, and age, Bossler and Holt included the respondent's level of self-control, and measures of respondent cyberdeviance and peer offending in their analyses. The authors reported that low self-control positively affected the likelihood of experiencing unauthorized password access, access and alteration of computer information or files, and online harassment. However, these effects disappeared once the cyberdeviance and peer offending measures were introduced into the models. The support for the lifestyle-routine activities perspective is two-fold. First, it appears that risky lifestyles increase victimization risk for online types of crimes just as they do offline. Second, the principle of homogamy makes a similar transition from offline to online realms. Regarding the effects of low self-control, the authors remarked: "These findings may indicate that individual characteristics and choice are less important in understanding certain forms of cybercrime victimization than others, particularly since some forms of cybercrime victimization can occur through no fault of the victim" (Bossler & Holt, 2010: 7). The current study will estimate the effects of online lifestyles and routines concurrently with the effects of low self-control on victimization.

Marcum's work has also contributed to the extant literature in which routine activity theory has been applied to college student cybervictimization (Marcum, 2009; Marcum et al., 2010a, 2010b). For her 2009 book, Marcum administered a self-report survey to freshman college students at a mid-sized university in the Northeast in order to examine the nature of their Internet use, especially as it affected their online victimization. Online victimization, the primary dependent variable, included online harassment, unwanted exposure to sexual material, and solicitation for sex. Marcum's (2009) study advanced the use of routine activities in cyberspace by measuring three of the core concepts of the theory (exposure to motivated offenders, target attractiveness, and guardianship). Exposure was measured by time spent online and the nature of online activities. Target attractiveness was conceptualized as actions taken on the part of the respondent that may have made them a more attractive target, such as providing personal information to online contacts. Guardianship was measured in ways similar to those of Choi (2008) and Holt and Bossler (2009) by asking respondents about their software protection, but also asking whether they physically had their Internet time restricted by a guardian, and whether they were monitored (by a guardian) while online.

Marcum's (2009) study consisted of two sets of analyses: one retrospective, asking students about their experiences as high school seniors, and one contemporary, asking respondents (as college freshmen) about their current experiences online. Those findings relevant to routine activities theory and its applicability to cyberspace yielded some conflicting effects. For instance, exposure and lack of guardianship both increased victimization risk for the online harassment dependent variable, but the presence of capable guardianship actually increased risk of receiving unwanted sexual materials. Regarding solicitation of sex, online guardianship again yielded unexpected results by increasing victimization risk[21]. Exposure also increased risk for the solicitation of

---

[21] Marcum (2009) has pointed out that the unexpected effects of guardianship on victimization may have been an artifact of question wording. Specifically,

sex. Marcum and her colleagues (2010a) republished these results in journal article form, but since there were no substantive differences between these studies, the later journal article will not be discussed in depth.

Marcum et al. (2010b) reanalyzed this same data from a gendered perspective, hypothesizing that online behaviors and routine activities may have different effects for men and women. For example, perhaps using Facebook increases likelihood of victimization for women, but not men. Although intriguing, and supported in the victimization literature (e.g., Henson et al., 2010; Holt & Bossler, 2009) this hypothesis was not truly tested by the authors because their male and female models included different variables. As an example, in estimating the likelihood of receiving unwanted and sexually explicit material during the college freshman time period, the authors examined the effects of using Facebook for females, but not males. This is rather like comparing apples and oranges. Nevertheless, the authors concluded that their measures of exposure and target attractiveness increased the likelihood of cybervictimization for both genders, while guardianship did not decrease the likelihood of victimization as expected.

Taken together, the studies reviewed above provide some preliminary support regarding the utility of lifestyle-routine activities theory in explaining online victimization, but more work is needed with respect to measuring key theoretical concepts. Without measures that adequately reflect the theoretical concepts, it is difficult to determine whether the theory is suited to explain cybercrimes. In considering the effects of exposure, proximity, target attractiveness, and guardianship across these studies, few patterns emerge. For example, the effects of exposure and guardianship are inconsistent across these studies, and the other elements of routine activity theory (e.g., suitable targets) were either not measured or had no demonstrable effect on victimization. Additional work in the area is needed to sort out the conflicting effects

---

restrictions on Internet use or presence of guardians during online routine activities may have been a consequence of previous online victimization and not a precursor to online victimization.

of the lifestyle-routine activities variables, and measures of specific online lifestyles will help to flesh out the effects of different lifestyles on victimization. Of course, these differences may be attributable to the different dependent variables of interest across these studies as well as differences in operationalization and measurement of the key theoretical concepts.

Studies of Other Populations
Although fewer in number, researchers have also utilized lifestyle-routine activities theory to explain the cybervictimization of adults in the general population (Pratt et al., 2010; Reyns, 2011; van Wilsem, 2011) and adolescents (Bossler et al., 2011). The first of these studies to be published focused on Internet fraud targeting among a sample of adults in the state of Florida (Pratt et al., 2010). Pratt and his colleagues conducted a telephone survey of 1,000 Florida residents, asking them about their experiences with consumer fraud and their Internet usage. The authors concluded that their measures of online routine activities, hours spent online and whether the respondent made a website purchase, were significantly related to fraud targeting. In other words, among members of the sample, individual online routines, both the amount of time spent online, and their remote purchasing behaviors, increased their likelihood of being targeted for fraud with the latter increasing this risk nearly four times. The finding that remote purchasing increases fraud targeting was echoed in another study by Holtfreter et al. (2008), in which remote purchasing increased both fraud targeting and fraud victimization. Although the measures of online routine activities from these studies were somewhat rudimentary in comparison to those utilized in other research, these studies are nonetheless important because they examined a large sample of adults rather than relying on a purposive or convenience sample of college students as so many other studies have. Further, these studies provide additional evidence that the routine activity perspective does indeed have value in accounting for crimes in which the victims and offenders are physically separated.

Reyns (2011) expanded on the idea that these place-based theories can explain crimes occurring at a distance by examining the impact of online routine activities on identity theft victimization. Utilizing a subsample of 5,985 respondents to the British Crime Survey, Reyns estimated the effects of 10 different online routines on victimization. In addition, since lifestyle-routine activities theory contends that the effects of individual characteristics such as sex, age, and race, should be mediated by lifestyles and daily routines, Reyns tested this proposition by estimating two statistical models: one containing only these types of individual characteristics, and a full model including individual characteristics and online routine activities, as well as offline routine activities and perceived risk of victimization. The 10 online routine activities included in the model measured whether the respondent used the Internet for: banking, shopping, email or instant messages, watching TV or listening to the radio, getting the news, participating in chat rooms or forums, reading or writing blogs, downloading media (e.g., music), social networking, or for work or study. In Reyns' first model, age, marital status, income and employment status all increased the likelihood that individuals would experience identity theft, with older individuals, those who were married, those with incomes above £50,000, and those who were employed being at increased risk. In the second model, the effects of age and income remained, and gender emerged as a significant indicator of victimization, with males being more likely to experience identity theft. In terms of the online routine activities variables, using the Internet for banking, shopping, email/instant messaging, and downloading media all significantly increased respondents' odds of victimization. Perceiving one's risk of victimization to be high had similar effects. This study further expanded support for argument that this place-based perspective is appropriate for crimes of physical and temporal separation.

Adding to this body of research, Bossler and his colleagues (2011) investigated the online harassment of juveniles from a routine activities perspective. Middle and high school students (N = 518) from two Kentucky schools participated in the study by taking an online survey designed by Bossler et al. to measure general computer use and online victimization. Online victimization was measured with four survey items tapping methods of online communication (e.g., email, instant message) that either made the respondent "feel bad," or "feel threatened or worried" (Bossler et al., 2011: 9). In terms of routine activity variables, the authors utilized hours online, whether the student used social networking sites, peer online harassment, computer deviance, and the respondent's online harassment of others as measures of proximity to motivated offenders. Guardianship was operationalized by considering physical guardianship (use of protective software), social guardianship (computer location and friends' deviance), and personal guardianship (computer skill level and risky information sharing). Target attractiveness was measured through proxies, including sex, race, academic standing, and report card grades. Variables from each of these routine activities concepts produced statistically significant relationships with victimization. Noteworthy findings from this study include: use of social networks, deviant peer associations, and sharing of sensitive information as precursors to the harassment victimization of adolescents.

CURRENT FOCUS

Taking into consideration this growing body of both cyberstalking and lifestyle-routine activities research, the purpose of the current study is: (1) to estimate the extent of cyberstalking amongst a random sample of college undergraduates at a large urban university in the Midwest; and, (2) to employ the lifestyle-routine activities perspective in an effort to better understand the correlates of this type of victimization. To this end, each of the lifestyle-routine activities concepts (exposure, proximity, target attractiveness, and guardianship), which are known indicators of college student victimization, have been adapted for operationalization within an online environment. Measures of *online exposure*, *online proximity*, *online target attractiveness*, and *online guardianship* have been constructed to test their relative effects on the cyberstalking victimization of college students.

Just as students may expose themselves to risky situations or come into physical proximity with motivated offenders in offline environments, they may also do so while online. For instance, the amount of time spent online engaged in various activities may be a measure of online exposure. Likewise, allowing strangers access to personal information online (e.g., adding strangers as "friends" to one's online social network) may affect one's likelihood of cyberstalking victimization via online proximity. Examples of online target attractiveness may be posting revealing information online such as photos, videos, or interests, and online guardianship may involve target hardening (e.g., restricting access to personal information). Other known correlates of victimization, online deviance and low self-control, will also be assessed for their role in influencing cyberstalking victimization.

The Theoretical Transition to Cyberspace 57

There is clearly a need for such an analysis considering that so much of past work into cyberstalking has been atheoretical and so little is known about lifestyles and routine activities as risk factors for cyberstalking victimization. Based on the previous review of the literature, support for the theoretical perspective as it applies to cybercrime victimization seems rather tepid. However, more work is needed before arriving at any conclusions regarding the explanatory power of the theory as it relates to cybercrimes.

This study expands upon past work and addresses issues which have not been fully explored. For instance, no study to date has considered a full lifestyle-routine activities model in the context of cyberstalking victimization while also taking into account the effects of delinquency and low self-control on victimization. Indeed, no other study of cyberstalking victimization has considered the role of self-control in precipitating victimization. Therefore, the current study fills these two gaps in the literature by addressing the role of low self-control and at the same time exploring all of the lifestyle-routine activities concepts simultaneously. In doing so, it is possible to identify risk factors for cyberstalking victimization. Knowing what places individuals at risk of cyberstalking victimization will be useful in crafting strategies for reducing cyberstalking opportunities, and consequently reducing the number of cyberstalking victims.

CHAPTER 4
Researching the Problem of Cyberstalking

As stated previously, the purposes of this study are threefold: (1) to estimate the extent of cyberstalking victimization among a sample of college students from a large urban university in the Midwest; (2) to utilize the lifestyle-exposure and routine activity theory perspectives to determine the correlates and risk factors for cyberstalking victimization (i.e., in terms of lifestyles and routine activities of college students); and, (3) to assess whether the lifestyle-routine activities perspective can successfully be adapted to explain victimization in virtual environments. Since few empirical estimates of cyberstalking have been published and most of these done rely heavily on nonprobability samples, the current study estimates of cyberstalking victimization represent an improvement over past work. These estimates are derived from a more methodologically solid research design than what has been utilized in many previous studies.

In addition, lifestyle-routine activities theory has not been applied to cybercrimes nearly to the extent that it has to other types of crime (e.g., personal, property), and thus far it has not been applied to the study of cyberstalking victimization. Doing so helps identify risk factors for cyberstalking victimization, and aids in crime prevention education and application aimed at reducing incidents of victimization. This theoretical approach has received considerable support in explaining place-based forms of crime (e.g., burglary), but there is much less certainty about its usefulness in explaining cybercrimes. The current study is among the first to address the issue of whether lifestyle-routine activities theory is restricted to explaining place-based forms of crime, or whether it has utility in explaining crimes in which traditional conceptions of place do not apply.

METHODS

The IRB Process and Obtaining Informed Consent

The Institutional Review Board (IRB) at the University of Cincinnati is charged with reviewing proposals for research to ensure that standards of ethical conduct are maintained during research studies in which human subjects are involved. The current study received IRB approval in November, 2008. IRB procedures mandate that researchers obtain informed consent from research subjects prior to their participation in any study. To comply with this rule, consent was obtained by including an informed consent form at the beginning of the questionnaire developed for the study. The form explained the purpose of the research study, the requirements and nature of participation (i.e., voluntary, anonymous), and provided information about the survey. The form also explained to participants that by proceeding with the completion of the survey they were indicating their consent for their answers to be used in the current research study. The informed consent form can be found in Appendix 2.

Sampling Design

The survey data were collected from students at a large urban public university in the Midwest. The study population consisted of those students possessing the following characteristics: enrolled in spring quarter 2009, undergraduate, between the ages of 18 and 24, attending the school at any of the university's campuses (i.e., the main campus, satellite campuses), and attending classes on a full-time basis. Once this group of students was identified, a simple random sample of 10,000 students out of a possible 16,592 was selected by the university registrar's office. To draw these 10,000 students at random, seven numbers were arbitrarily chosen. Those students whose student ID number ended in one of those seven numbers were selected for inclusion, and this process continued until 10,000 students had been selected. The student population was not sorted on any criterion, so the listing of sample members was completely random.

Data Collection

During April and May 2009, the sample of students was sent emails through the university registrar's office inviting them to participate in a web-based survey. The survey was administered through a survey software tool called Zoomerang which allows subscribers to design and host online surveys using their software and servers for a monthly fee. Students who decided to participate in the survey were instructed to visit the web link included in the invitation email, at which point they were taken to the online survey.

Three waves of invitation emails were sent out to the original group of 10,000 students over the course of approximately five weeks. A follow-up invitation was sent to the group after two weeks, and a third and final invite was sent after another two weeks. Following Dillman's (2007) *Tailored Design Method*, the content of each email invitation was varied slightly across these three waves in an attempt to elicit a higher response rate from students. This method focuses on establishing trust, arousing interest in the survey, reducing the perceived costs of participation, and increasing the perceived rewards of participation. This latter point was particularly delicate given IRB restrictions on providing benefits to respondents. In an effort to follow Dillman's (2007) suggestions, the language of the email invitation was revised from wave to wave. For example, the final email invitation indicated that it would be the last time that the student would be requested to participate, and reiterated the importance of their participation in attaining an adequate number of usable surveys. These three invitation emails are provided in Appendix 3, 4, and 5.

Response Rate

Of the initial 10,000 students who were sent emails, 74 emails were returned as undeliverable (e.g., email address was not valid), making the sample size of invitees who could potentially participate in the study 9,926. The response rate across all three waves of invitations is difficult to calculate, because there is no way of knowing how many of the 9,926 invitations were received, opened, or read by the intended recipients. A conservative estimate of the response rate based on the assumption that all of these invitations were delivered and read would be 13.2%[22]. This equates to 751 completed surveys and an additional 563 partially completed surveys.

These partially completed surveys were in varying stages of completeness. For instance, some of the partials were designated as such because the respondent did not submit the survey properly (even though they may have answered all of the survey questions), and as a result were labeled as incomplete by the survey software. This scenario could have occurred if respondents reached the end of the survey and closed their web browser without clicking the "submit survey" tab. On the other end of the spectrum, there were other partially completed surveys that had virtually no data provided by the respondent. For instance, a respondent may have followed the web link to the survey, answered only the first question, and exited the survey. After these cases with significant amounts of missing data were removed from the sample (i.e., respondents only answered the first few questions), the sample size decreased to 1,252.

A less conservative estimate of the response rate can be calculated based on the number of students known to have received their invitations. This estimate is based on the group who opened their invitations and subsequently followed the web link to the informed consent form.

---

[22] By conventional survey methodology standards, this is a quite low rate of participation; however, it is not unusual considering the population under study, the lack of incentives for respondents to participate, the mode of administration, and the generally high level of competition for "Internet time" from spam emails, other Internet surveys, university announcements, and the like. Couper (2000) has explained that in comparison to other modes of survey administration (e.g., mail, phone), web surveys often attain lower rates of participation (e.g., under 10% for single invitation surveys). Further, in Dillman et al.'s (2009) comparison of response rates of mixed-mode surveys, the authors reported that response rates varied widely across mode of administration (mail, telephone, interactive voice response, Internet). For instance, the response rate for mail surveys was the highest at 75%, while the response rate for the web survey was the lowest at 12.7%. The response rate for the current study is therefore not surprising considering no incentives were provided to respondents (as they were in Dillman et al.'s study), and the generally low rates of participation in similar studies of comparable populations (e.g., Hilinski, 2009; Nobles et al., 2009).

Of these individuals, 67.1% completed the survey. Narrowing it down further, considering only the students who began the survey and answered at least the first question, the response rate would equate to 76.8%.

Missing Data Issues
Potential missing data problems required deleting additional cases for which no data were provided by respondents on the dependent variables. Allison (2001) has suggested that cases with missing values may be treated with a variety of statistical techniques, including listwise deletion, pairwise deletion, mean substitution, maximum likelihood estimation, multiple imputation, and others; however, he argues that none of these techniques are advisable for missing data on dependent variables (Allison, 2001; see also Little and Rubin, 2002). In the survey instrument used to gather data for the current study, many of the dependent variables appeared toward the end of the questionnaire, which unfortunately means that as cases were lost to attrition the majority of the missing data were missing on the dependent variables. Following Allison's advice (personal communication, July 10, 2009), cases were deleted that were missing data on the four cyberstalking victimization variables (the primary dependent variables) and the identity fraud victimization variable. By deleting these cases, an additional 278 cases were lost, making the final sample size 974.

Sample Characteristics
The sample consisted of 974 undergraduate students attending school full time during spring of 2009, and possessed the following characteristics: a majority of respondents were female (61%), white (86%), and the mean age of respondents was 20.22 years. In addition, 93.9% of sample respondents indicated they were heterosexual/straight, and the majority of respondents were either single (42.2%) or in a serious/long-term dating relationship (40.2%); the remainder of respondents were casually dating (12.7%) or married/living with someone (4.5%). With respect to where students lived during the school year, most were living off-campus in non-university housing (46.7%), followed by on-campus

housing (23.2%), in the home of a parent, guardian or relative (23.1%), or in off-campus university housing (7.1%). A majority of students lived with a student roommate (60.9%), and 8.5% lived alone. Fraternity or sorority members made up 12% of the sample, and university athletic team members made up 7.4%.

Table 4.1 provides select sample characteristics and population characteristics which were provided by the university registrar's office.

Table 4.1: Select Sample and Population Characteristics[23]

Demographic Characteristics	Sample Statistics		University Population Characteristics	
	Percentage	N	Percentage	N
Gender				
Male	39%	379	51.3%	8,200
Female	61%	593	48.7%	7,786
Age				
18	7.7%	75	6.5%	1,053
19	25.9%	252	23.8%	3,805
20	27.1%	264	22.7%	3,639
21	21.7%	211	18.6%	2,979
22	13.1%	128	15.6%	2,495
23	2.9%	28	8.7%	1,403
24	1.6%	16	3.8%	612
Race				
White	86%	828	80.3%	12,830
Black	6%	58	8.9%	1,423
Asian	3.2%	31	3.4%	555
Hispanic	1.6%	15	1.4%	226
Other	3.2%	31	5.9%	952

Note: The mean age and (standard deviation) for the sample are 20.22 ($s = 1.34$) and for the larger university sample are 20.54 ($s = 1.59$).

It is evident upon examining Table 4.1 that some demographic characteristics of the sample are quite different than the characteristics of the population from which it was drawn. In terms of gender, for

---

[23] As of May 18, 2009.

instance, the population was comprised of 51.3% males and 48.7% females, but the final sample of students who participated in the study was 39% male and 61% female. In terms of age and race, the differences between the population and the sample are much less substantial. The sample is overrepresentative of whites, and the youngest members of the population (i.e., 18 - 21 year olds), and underrepresentative of blacks and those in the 22 - 24 age group. Those who identified themselves as Asian or Hispanic closely match their percentages in the university student population.

Survey Instrument
Construction of the survey instrument began in the early months of 2007 and continued for more than two years following Dillman's (2007) and Dillman, Smyth, and Christian's (2008) *Tailored Design Method*. The final incident-based survey instrument is located in Appendix 6 and contains an individual-level questionnaire and an incident-level questionnaire. The surveys were designed to measure the extent of student victimization and to collect other relevant information such as demographics, lifestyles, and routine activity patterns. In terms of organization, the questionnaire was divided into three main parts: (1) demographics and lifestyle questions; (2) questions about online social network usage; and, (3) questions pertaining to other online routine activities (e.g., website visitation) and victimization (i.e., cyberstalking experiences). The length of time it took to complete the survey varied from respondent to respondent, but in general should not have taken much longer than 15-25 minutes.

It is difficult to say exactly how many items the questionnaire contains because of skip patterns and contingency questions. The number of answers a respondent would be asked to provide depended upon how they answered previous questions, in particular those questions related to cyberstalking victimization. For instance, respondents who indicated they had been the recipient of unwanted sexual advances online on more than one occasion were asked to report how many different people made unwanted sexual advances toward them (i.e., 1-4 people, 5 or more people). The number of offenders reported by the respondent corresponded with the number of incident reports they were asked to fill out, up to five reports. These incident reports contained nine questions each asking respondents to disclose details of the incident such as how the respondent knew that person, how long they had known that person, and the consequences of the incident.

Pilot Test

In the course of developing the survey instrument, a pilot test of the questionnaire and the survey software was conducted. During fall quarter 2007 (late November), the online survey was administered to a group of about 40 criminal justice students seeking master's degrees at the university. There were two advantages of pilot testing the questionnaire on these students: first, they were not eligible for inclusion in the final sample; and second, they were (for the most part) recently undergraduates, so their interpretation of the questions and format of the survey should have closely approximated an "undergrad's" perceptions. As part of the pilot test, the group was divided into three subgroups; each student was assigned a different "role" to cover all possible stalking scenarios (e.g., repeatedly contacted, but not harassed, threatened, sexually harassed, targeted for identify theft). After the students had taken the questionnaire, each group met as a focus group with the author and the co-investigator to discuss their experiences with the survey content and administration. Based on feedback from these students, the questionnaire was further revised.

Dependent Variables: Cyberstalking Victimization and Identity Fraud

As noted above, cyberstalking victimization is the primary dependent variable. Cyberstalking victimization is defined as repeated pursuit (two or more occasions) of the victim by the perpetrator using electronic devices or the Internet. There are four types of pursuit behaviors that each represent a different form of cyberstalking victimization. These elements can occur together, or singly, but if any or all of them have taken place, a cyberstalking victimization incident has occurred. Each of these four victimization indicators was measured as a dichotomous variable (0 = No, 1 = Yes), representing whether or not the respondent had ever (in their lifetime) experienced any one of the four types of cyberstalking victimization. These four types of cyberstalking victimization include: (1) having been contacted repeatedly after asking the other party to stop; (2) having been repeatedly harassed or annoyed; (3)

having repeatedly been the recipient of unwanted sexual advances; or, (4) having been repeatedly threatened with violence. In addition, previous research (e.g., Bocij, 2003; Jerin & Dolinsky, 2001) has suggested that identity fraud victimization, such as having one's identity assumed online, is a form of cyberstalking. However, identity fraud is qualitatively different than these four forms of cyberstalking because it is not necessarily a crime of repeated pursuit. For this reason, identity fraud is measured in the current study, but is not included as one of the pursuit behaviors comprising cyberstalking victimization. Appendix 7 lists the survey items used to construct each dependent, independent, and control variable.

The possibility of creating a multi-item cyberstalking victimization scale was explored. A reliability analysis that included all four measures yielded an unacceptably low Cronbach's alpha (0.473). In fact, no combination of the variables resulted in an acceptable reliability statistic[24]. This result suggests that while each of these four pursuit behaviors may be labeled *cyberstalking*, they are indicators of four distinct types of pursuit by the perpetrator. A composite measure of cyberstalking based on the four types of cyberstalking victimization was created, indicating whether or not the respondent had ever[25] been a victim of any of the four types of cyberstalking. This measure was coded as a dichotomous variable (0 = Never experienced cyberstalking, 1 = experienced at least one type of cyberstalking). For instance, if the respondent indicated they had been the recipient of only unwanted sexual advances, they would be assigned a value of 1; likewise, someone who had experienced all four types of victimization would also be assigned a value of 1; only those respondents who did not experience any of the four types of cyberstalking were assigned a score of 0. Table 4.2 provides the descriptive statistics for these six dependent variables.

---

[24] Typically, a Cronbach's alpha over 0.60 would indicate favorable conditions for scale construction.

[25] Estimates generated in the current study will measure lifetime prevalence of victimization.

Independent Variables: Measures of Online Lifestyles/Routine Activities

Based on responses to the victimization survey, measures of each of the lifestyle-routine activities concepts (online exposure, online guardianship, online proximity, and online target attractiveness) were constructed. The operationalization of online delinquency and low self-control are also discussed below.

Online Exposure

Traditionally, the concept of exposure has been measured by examining the non-household activities of study participants (e.g., the number of nights out) under the assumption that more time out of the home equates to greater exposure to risk of victimization (e.g., Cohen et al., 1981; Miethe & Meier, 1994). In studies focused upon college students, exposure has been operationalized in terms of public behaviors and in terms of presence in risky environments (i.e., presence of alcohol or drugs) (Fisher, et al., 2002; Mustaine & Tewksbury, 1999). A similar measure for online exposure is problematic as one can just as easily engage in online activities at home as they can anywhere else.

Table 4.2: Cyberstalking and Identity Fraud Victimization Variables

Dependent Variables	Scale	Mean	SD	Range	N
Single-Item Measures of Cyberstalking Victimization and Identity Fraud					
Contacted	(0 = No, 1 = Yes)	0.23	0.42	0 – 1	974
Harassed	(0 = No, 1 = Yes)	0.20	0.40	0 – 1	964
Sexual Advances	(0 = No, 1 = Yes)	0.14	0.34	0 – 1	953
Violently Threatened	(0 = No, 1 = Yes)	0.04	0.20	0 – 1	942
Identity Fraud	(0 = No, 1 = Yes)	0.11	0.31	0 – 1	943
Four-Item Composite Measure					
Cyberstalking	(0 = No, 1 = Yes)	0.41	0.49	0 – 1	974

However, the main idea of increased exposure to risk can be adapted to fit online environments. The concept of *online exposure* was operationalized using six of the survey questions asking respondents about how much time they spend online, and in what online activities they participate (i.e., social networks, blogs) that might reveal information about them. These six measures of online exposure include: (1) how much time the respondent spends online each day (measured as a count of hours); (2) how many social networks/blogs the respondent has (measured as a count of SNs); (3) how many times a week the respondent updates the information on their social network/blog (measured as a count of updates); (4) how many hours a day the respondent spends on their social network/blog (measured as a count of hours); (5) how many photos the respondent has posted on their social network/blog (measured as a count of photos); and, (6) whether they regularly use AOL Instant Messenger (measured as a dichotomy, 0 = No, 1 = Yes). Descriptive statistics for the online exposure variables are provided in Table 4.3.

Table 4.3: Online Exposure Variables

Exposure Variables	Scale	Mean	SD	Range	N
Time Online	(Time in hours per day)	3.93	3.93	1 – 16	969
Number of Social Networks	(Number of SNs)	2.60	1.70	1 – 15	901
Number of SN Updates	(Number of updates per week)	2.41	3.85	0 – 25	906
Time on Social Network	(Number of hours per day)	1.58	1.72	1 – 16	904
Number Photos on SN	(Number of photos)	350.37	466.76	0 – 5000	880
Use AOL Instant Messenger	(0 = No, 1 = Yes)	0.35	0.48	0 – 1	974

Online Guardianship
Prior research has often focused upon two dimensions of guardianship, the physical and the social (e.g., Mustaine & Tewksbury, 1998; Newman, 1996; Wilcox Rountree & Land, 1996; Sampson & Wooldredge, 1987; Tewksbury & Mustaine, 2003). The physical dimension of guardianship has been measured in previous work by examining various aspects of target hardening such as locking doors, the presence of dogs, and police patrols. These precautions are unlikely to have any effect on cybervictimization; however, the idea that active guardianship discourages victimization can be adapted for use in online environments. Choi's (2008) and Holt and Bossler's (2009) studies of college student cybervictimization operationalized guardianship in terms of students' security features on their computer (e.g., presence of firewalls, anti-virus software). Unfortunately, measures of the presence of firewalls and security programs are not available in the current data. The guardianship measures that are available may be more applicable to cyberstalking victimization because firewalls and security programs for the most part do not protect against repeated contact or pursuit behaviors (i.e., they are designed to protect against malicious software, and not routine online activities). In the current study, the physical aspect of guardianship is measured by two variables: (1) whether the respondent has their online social network/blog account set to private or limited access; and, (2) whether they use or have used a profile tracker that keeps track of who views their account. Each of these two items is measured as a dichotomy (0 = No, 1 = Yes). These measures are potentially limited in that they are both premised on the respondent currently or previously using a social network or blog account. However, 96.3% of the sample had a social network or blog at the time of the survey or prior to the survey, so these measures of guardianship are applicable to the vast majority of students in the sample. Table 4.4 provides descriptive statistics for the online guardianship variables.

Table 4.4: Online Guardianship Variables

Guardianship Variables	Scale	Mean	SD	Range	N
SN Set to Private	(0 = No, 1 = Yes)	0.82	0.38	0 – 1	906
Use a Profile Tracker	(0 = No, 1 = Yes)	0.12	0.33	0 – 1	907

Online Proximity

The proximity to crime element of routine activities theory represents the potential target's physical proximity to motivated offenders. Prior work examining college students' victimization has operationalized this theoretical concept in terms of routine activities that bring potential targets into physical proximity with motivated offenders (e.g., Cass, 2007). Because cybercrimes do not involve the physical convergence of victims and offenders, this concept needs to be adapted to fit virtual environments. As Eck and Clarke (2003) have pointed out, victims and offenders need not necessarily converge in physical space. There are a number of crimes (e.g., mail bombings, harassing phone calls, health care fraud) in which victims and offenders come together through a network. While the authors do not specifically address the idea of proximity to motivated offenders vis-à-vis the network, it seems reasonable that proximity may be adapted to include greater proximity to offenders via the network. This is the approach taken in the current study to operationalize online proximity. Accordingly, three measures of online proximity have been developed: (1) whether the respondent has ever added someone as "friend" on their online social network whom they didn't know (i.e., a stranger); (2) how many "friends" in total the respondent has across all of their online social networks; and, (3) whether the respondent has ever joined an online service that assisted them in acquiring new "friends" for their online social network. Table 4.5 presents the descriptive statistics for the online proximity variables.

Table 4.5: Online Proximity Variables

Proximity Variables	Scale	Mean	SD	Range	N
Added Stranger as Friend	(0 = No, 1 = Yes)	0.72	0.45	0 – 1	907
Number of Friends on SN	(Number of friends)	513.50	524.73	7 – 5000	887
Friend Service	(0 = No, 1 = Yes)	0.03	0.18	0 – 1	903

Online Target Attractiveness

According to Cohen et al. (1981: 508), target attractiveness is "the material or symbolic desirability of persons or property targets to potential offenders, as well as the perceived inertia of a target against illegal treatment." This means that a target might appear attractive to a potential offender if it has some value to the offender or if it easily targeted (e.g., the weight of something makes it easy to remove, a person does not have the capacity to resist an attack). As noted above, Clarke (1999) has also argued that hot products, or those products that are repeatedly targeted, are CRAVED (i.e., Concealable, Removable, Available, Valuable, Enjoyable, and Disposable). Newman and Clarke (2003) have further argued that information such as social security numbers or credit card numbers have CRAVED attributes. Depending upon the crime, different types of information may be attractive targets for offenders. In the context of college student victimization, previous research operationalized target attractiveness as the possession of cash as disposable income (Fisher et al., 1998). These are not ideal measures of online target attractiveness, as a would-be stalker is not likely to have any knowledge of a target's material wealth. In the case of cyberstalking, any information that facilitates the pursuit of the victim (e.g., email addresses, phone numbers) or discloses details about the potential victim (e.g., sexual orientation, photos) may make the target more attractive, at least to stranger stalkers. The current study utilizes nine indicators of target attractiveness based on the type of information respondents may have posted/provided on their online profiles (i.e., online social network, blog) including: (1) their full name; (2) their relationship status; (3) their sexual orientation; (4) their instant messenger ID; (5) their email address; (6) address for other social network/blog sites; (7) interests and/or activities; (8) photos; and, (9) videos. Each of these nine items was measured as a dichotomy (0 = No, 1 = Yes). A composite measure of online target attractiveness was created based upon the respondent's mean level of attractiveness. To compensate for any missing values on these nine indicators, only respondents who answered four of the nine questions were included in the calculation of the composite variable. Table 4.6 provides descriptive statistics for the online target attractiveness variables.

Table 4.6: Online Target Attractiveness Variables

Target Attractiveness Variables	Scale	Mean	SD	Range	N
Full Name	(0 = No, 1 = Yes)	0.71	0.45	0 – 1	974
Relationship Status	(0 = No, 1 = Yes)	0.77	0.42	0 – 1	974
Sexual Orientation	(0 = No, 1 = Yes)	0.67	0.47	0 – 1	974
Instant Messenger	(0 = No, 1 = Yes)	0.37	0.48	0 – 1	974
Email Address	(0 = No, 1 = Yes)	0.65	0.47	0 – 1	974
Other SN Addresses	(0 = No, 1 = Yes)	0.09	0.28	0 – 1	974
Interests/Activities	(0 = No, 1 = Yes)	0.74	0.44	0 – 1	974
Photos	(0 = No, 1 = Yes)	0.88	0.32	0 – 1	974
Videos	(0 = No, 1 = Yes)	0.36	0.48	0 – 1	974
Composite Measure	(Mean target attractiveness)	0.58	0.23	0 – 1	974

Online Deviance

A strong relationship between deviant behavior and/or delinquency and victimization is consistently reported in studies of victimization (e.g., Lauritsen, Laub & Sampson, 1992; Lauritsen, Sampson & Laub, 1991; Sampson & Lauritsen, 1990). In the present study, online deviance is measured with eight items representing different deviant acts. Each of the eight items was measured as a dichotomy (0 = No, 1 = Yes). Respondents were asked if they have participated in any of the following activities: (1) repeatedly contacted or attempted to contact someone online after they asked/told you to stop; (2) repeatedly harassed or annoyed someone online after they asked/told you to stop; (3) repeatedly made unwanted sexual advances toward someone; (4) repeatedly spoken to someone in a violent manner or threatened to physically harm them online after they asked/told you to stop; (5) attempted to hack into someone's online social network account; (6) downloaded music or movies illegally; (7) sent sexually explicit images to someone online or through text messaging; and, (8) received sexually explicit images from someone online or through text messaging. Table 4.7 provides the descriptive statistics for the online deviance variables.

Similar to the online target attractiveness measure, a composite measure of the respondent's mean online deviance was created. Once again, to compensate for any missing values on these indicators of online deviance, only respondents who answered four of the eight questions pertaining to deviance were included in the calculation of the composite variable. Descriptive statistics for this composite measure appear in Table 4.7.

Table 4.7: Online Deviance Variables

Deviance Variables	Scale	Mean	SD	Range	N
Contacted someone	(0 = No, 1 = Yes)	0.03	0.17	0 – 1	791
Harassed someone	(0 = No, 1 = Yes)	0.02	0.15	0 – 1	791
Unwanted Sexual Advances	(0 = No, 1 = Yes)	0.01	0.08	0 – 1	791
Threatened someone	(0 = No, 1 = Yes)	0.01	0.10	0 – 1	791
Hack	(0 = No, 1 = Yes)	0.13	0.34	0 – 1	791
Illegal downloads	(0 = No, 1 = Yes)	0.65	0.47	0 – 1	791
Sent explicit images	(0 = No, 1 = Yes)	0.24	0.43	0 – 1	791
Received explicit images	(0 = No, 1 = Yes)	0.38	0.48	0 – 1	791
Eight-Item Composite Measure					
Online Deviance	(Mean level of deviance)	0.19	0.18	0 – 1	791

Low Self-Control

According to Gottfredson and Hirschi (1990), once the effects of low self-control are considered in predicting crime and other negative life outcomes (e.g., deviance, victimization), other predictors in the statistical models become spurious. For example, target attractiveness may be a robust predictor of cyberstalking victimization if the effect of low self-control is not considered; however, the elements of target attractiveness that make one more likely to be victimized can really be traced back to the individual's self-control. In this scenario, low self-control may affect one's likelihood to post sexually provocative photos online or describe drug and drinking habits on their blog (behaviors that may signal an attractive target to potential offenders). Therefore, once this underlying trait is taken into account, target attractiveness should no longer be as robust a predictor of victimization. For these reasons, it is important to consider the role of low self-control in explaining cyberstalking victimization.

The current study utilizes a single measure of low self-control based upon four survey items. Respondents were asked how strongly they agreed with statements measuring a propensity toward low self-control, including "I consider myself to be argumentative," "I have trouble controlling my temper," "I often confront people when they make me upset," and "I consider myself to be a risk-taker." These four statements were rated by respondents with values on the items ranging from 1 ("strongly agree") to 4 ("strongly disagree"), so higher scores indicate a higher propensity toward self-control. These scales were reversed to reflect lower self-control at higher scores (i.e., 4 = low self-control). Descriptive statistics for the self-control survey items appear in Table 4.8. These four items were combined into a single measure of low self-control with a Cronbach's α of 0.55. This alpha is somewhat low by conventional standards for scale construction and presents a potential limitation to the study's findings related to the effects of low self-control, but if the measure performs as expected it can be thought of as conservative estimation of the effects of low self-control on cyberstalking victimization.

Table 4.8: Self-Control Survey Items

Self-Control Variables	Scale	Mean	SD	Range	N
Argumentative	(1 = Strongly Disagree to 4 = Strongly Agree)	2.51	0.88	1 – 4	974
Trouble Controlling Temper	(1 = Strongly Disagree to 4 = Strongly Agree)	1.73	0.77	1 – 4	974
Confront those who Upset Me	(1 = Strongly Disagree to 4 = Strongly Agree)	2.51	0.78	1 – 4	974
Risk-Taker	(1 = Strongly Disagree to 4 = Strongly Agree)	2.46	0.78	1 – 4	974
Multi-Item Measure					
Low Self-Control	(1 = More Self-Control to 4 = Low Self-Control)	2.30	0.52	1 – 4	974

Another possible limitation exists in the items used to construct this measure of low self-control. Namely, the standard for measuring low self-control was set by Grasmick, Tittle, Bursik, and Arneklev (1993) in their assessment of Gottfredson and Hirschi's (1990) general theory of crime. The authors utilized a 24-item scale to measure this latent trait. This scale was not utilized in the current study, although many of the core concepts are represented in the self-control survey items (i.e., risk-taking, low tolerance for frustration). This presents a potential limitation to study findings; however, this is not a fatal shortcoming, as other researchers (e.g., Schreck et al., 2002; Schreck et al., 2006) have measured low self-control without utilizing the entirety of Grasmick et al.'s scale. Further, Pratt and Cullen (2000: 952), upon conducting a meta-analysis of studies estimating the effects of low self-control on offending, concluded that self-control was one of the most robust predictors of crime; they observed further that "…the effect size was not significantly affected by whether self-control was measured by an attitudinal or behavioral measure or whether it was measured by Grasmick et al.'s (1993) scale or by scales developed by other scholars." The authors argued that "This latter finding is important because it suggests that self-control's effects are sufficiently robust that they are not sensitive to different ways in which self-control is operationalized," (Pratt & Cullen, 2000: 952).

Control Variables
The effects of respondent demographics, associations with deviant peers, and participation in risky offline lifestyles are statistically controlled for in the analyses given the influence these variables have exhibited in previous victimization research.

Demographics
Previous victimization research has identified certain demographic characteristics as potentially important predictors of victimization (e.g., Fisher et al., 1998; Hindelang et al., 1978; Miethe & Meier, 1994; Rand, 2008; Sampson, 1987). In line with previous research, the following demographic characteristics will be included as control variables: race (0 = white, 1 = nonwhite), sex (0 = male, 1 = female), and respondent's age (measured in years). Relationship status will also be included as a control variable in the analysis (0 = not single, 1 = single).

Deviant Peers
It is also necessary to control for the influence of peer associations in the form of "delinquent" or "deviant" friends as previous research suggests that these associations may represent proximity to motivated offenders as well as less-than-capable guardianship (e.g., Jensen & Brownfield, 1986; Lauritsen et al., 1991; Schreck et al., 2006; Wilcox, Tillyer & Fisher, 2009). A measure of deviant peers was created based on three survey responses to the following survey item: "How likely do you think it is a friend or acquaintance will use the information on your social network/blog to do any of the following?" Respondents rated the likelihood of three forms of online pursuit by peers—namely, harassment, stalking, and threats of physical harm. Item responses for each ranged from not likely at all (1) to very likely (10). A single measure representing these three responses yielded a Cronbach's α of 0.80.

Risky Offline Activities
A large body of empirical evidence points to risky lifestyles and routine activities as correlates of a variety of types of offline victimization (e.g., Fisher et al., 1998; Jensen & Brownfield, 1986; Henson et al., 2010; Lasley, 1989; Miethe, Stafford, & Sloane, 1990; Mustaine & Tewksbury, 1998; Sampson & Lauritsen, 1990; Sampson & Wooldredge, 1987). However, it is unclear whether these types of risky offline activities increase one's chances of online victimization. To control for the effects of risky offline activities, a measure based on three survey items was created. These three survey items appear in Appendix 7, and measure the students' frequency of party attendance, bar and night club patronage, and alcohol consumption. The Cronbach's α for these three items is 0.67.

STATISTICAL TECHNIQUES

Bivariate and multivariate analyses were conducted to explore the relationships between the independent, dependent, and control variables. The statistical techniques for assessing these relationships are discussed below.

Bivariate Analyses

Bivariate relationships between the independent variables and between the independent and dependent variables will be calculated and presented in the next chapter. Two types of statistics will be used to represent the strength and direction of the relationships between these variables, point biserial correlation coefficients (r_{pb}) and Phi coefficients (φ). The point biserial correlation coefficient is essentially a special case of Pearson's r in which one of the variables in the relationship is nominal and dichotomous and the other is continuous. Phi coefficients are generated using chi-square and are appropriate to use as a measure of association when both variables in the bivariate relationship are nominal and dichotomous. In the case of both statistics, their interpretation is the same as the Pearson product-moment correlation coefficient (Pearson's r) (Field, 2005).

Multivariate Analyses

As noted, each of the four cyberstalking victimization variables (contact, harass, sexual advances, and threats of violence) have been measured as dichotomies (0 = No, 1 = Yes). Identity fraud, and the overall cyberstalking victimization measure, which simply measures whether the respondent answered affirmatively to any of the four cyberstalking questions, are also dichotomous (0 = No, 1 = Yes). The dichotomous nature of the dependent variables makes binary logistic regression the appropriate multivariate technique to explore the relationships between the lifestyle-routine activities variables and the cyberstalking victimization variables (Pampel, 2000). According to Pampel (2000: 18), this technique can be described as "regression on a dependent variable that transforms nonlinear relationships into linear relationships." After estimating logistic regression models, it is customary to report model fit statistics (i.e., -2 log likelihood, model chi square), as well as log-odds (B), Exp(B) (odds ratios), and standard errors. In logistic regression, the coefficients are represented by the (B) statistic, and characterize the nature of the relationship between the independent variables and the dependent variable. Since these coefficients are presented as log-odds, their interpretation is not intuitive. For that reason, odds ratios, which are easier to interpret, are calculated and reported. Coefficients with *p*-values less than 0.05 will be considered statistically significant, meaning that the null hypothesis can be rejected at the alpha 0.05 level.

CHAPTER 5
The Extent and Nature of Cyberstalking Victimization

RESULTS

This chapter presents three sets of results. First, the extent of cyberstalking victimization among members of the sample is reported. Lifetime prevalence of victimization and the characteristics of victims are reported for each type of cyberstalking victimization, identity fraud victimization, and the composite cyberstalking victimization measure. Second, bivariate analyses and results are briefly discussed. Correlations between the independent and dependent variables were initially calculated to explore the nature of these relationships and to inform the multivariate analyses. Third, binary logistic regression models that estimate the effects of the independent variables – online lifestyle-routine activities, online delinquency, and low self-control – on each of the dependent variables are presented and discussed. The dependent variables in question are: unwanted contact, harassment, unwanted sexual advances, threats of violence, identity fraud, and overall cyberstalking victimization.

EXTENT OF VICTIMIZATION

Lifetime Prevalence of Victimization by Types of Pursuit

Figure 5.1 illustrates the lifetime prevalence of cyberstalking victimization across the four types of pursuit behaviors (i.e., contact, harassment, sexual advances, violent threats), identity fraud, and overall cyberstalking. Among sample members, the prevalence of cyberstalking victimization was 40.8% ($N = 397$).

Across types of online pursuit behaviors, repeated contact was the most frequent method of cyberstalking, with over 23.3% (*N* = 227) of the sample having such an experience. The next most frequent method of cyberstalking experienced by respondents was repeated harassment, with 20.1% (*N* = 196) of the sample experiencing online harassment, followed by unwanted sexual advances at 13.9% (*N* = 132). Identity fraud (having someone else pose as the victim online) was experienced by 10.6% (*N* = 100) of respondents, and threats of violence through electronic communications was experienced by the fewest respondents with 4.4% (*N* = 41) of the sample being threatened online.

Figure 5.1: Percentage of Respondents who Experienced Online Victimization

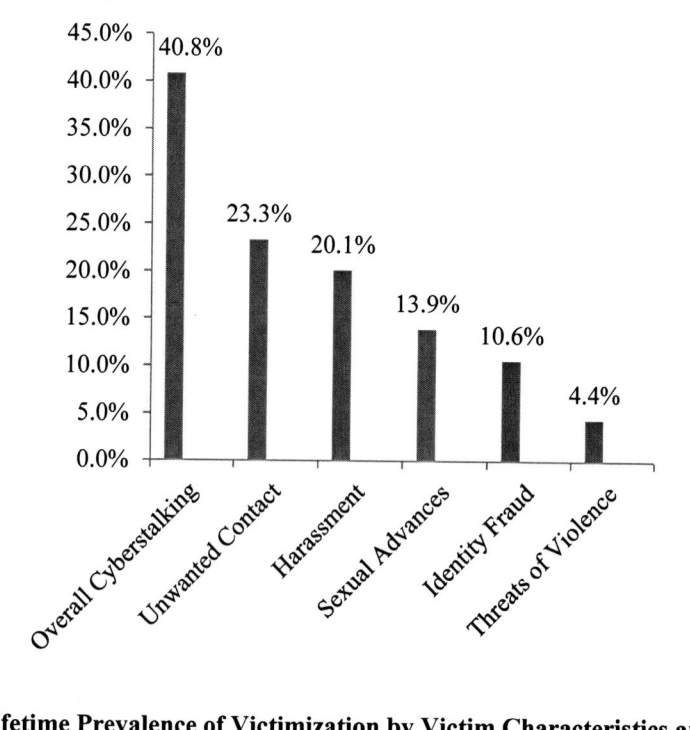

Category	Percentage
Overall Cyberstalking	40.8%
Unwanted Contact	23.3%
Harassment	20.1%
Sexual Advances	13.9%
Identity Fraud	10.6%
Threats of Violence	4.4%

Lifetime Prevalence of Victimization by Victim Characteristics and Types of Online Victimization

Demographic characteristics have long been identified as consistent correlates of a variety of types of victimization (e.g., Cohen et al., 1981; Hindelang et al., 1978; Rand, 2008; Wilcox et al., 2009). Therefore, demographic characteristics such as sex, age, race, and relationship status are considered in current estimates of the extent of victimization amongst members of the sample. Table 5.1 presents the extent of victimization broken down by: sex, age (under 21/21 and over) race (white/nonwhite), and relationship status (single/non-single). In addition, extent of victimization among certain groups (e.g., white females, single males) is reported in Table 5.2.

Sex
Table 5.1 summarizes the extent of cyberstalking victimization among males and females in the sample across types of cyberstalking victimization and identity fraud. A higher percentage of sample females were victimized compared to sample males for unwanted contact, harassment, sexual advances, and overall cyberstalking, and as the results reported in Table 5.1 illustrate, each of these differences in victimization between males and females is statistically significant. For the composite cyberstalking measure, 46.3% of females were cyberstalked compared to 32.1% of males: χ^2 (1, $N = 972$) = 19.27, $p \leq 0.01$. For unwanted contact, 27.9% of female respondents were victimized compared to 16.1% of their male counterparts: χ^2 (1, $N = 972$) = 18.12, $p \leq 0.01$. Regarding harassment, 25.2% of females were victimized compared to 12.9% of males: χ^2 (1, $N = 962$) = 21.37, $p \leq 0.01$. For sexual advances, 18% of female respondents were victimized, while 7.5% of males had such an experience: χ^2 (1, $N = 951$) = 21.08, $p \leq 0.01$. Slightly more males than females were threatened with violence through electronic communications (5.4% compared to 3.7%), but this 1.7% difference in victimization between males and females is not statistically significant: χ^2 (1, $N = 940$) = 1.56, $p = 0.41$. Finally, the percentage of males and females in the sample who experienced identity fraud was equal, with 10.6% of both men and women having had someone pose as them online.

Age
Table 5.1 also presents the extent of cyberstalking victimization by age (under 21/21 or older) across types of online pursuit and identity fraud.

Respondents in the under 21 years age group experienced slightly more overall cyberstalking victimization than did those in the 21 years and over age group (42.1% compared to 38.6%), although the difference is not statistically significant: χ^2 (1, N = 974) = 1.17, p = 0.15. For the other dependent variables, amount of victimization across age groups (under 21 years, 21 years and over) are also fairly comparable. For instance, 20.6% of those under 21 experienced harassment, while 19.8% of those 21 and older were harassed. There are no statistically significant differences in victimization across age groups for any of the types of cyberstalking victimization or identity fraud victimization ($\alpha \leq$ 0.05).

Table 5.2 illustrates the extent of cyberstalking victimization across sex and age categories. The results indicate that females under 21 years old experienced the most victimization, followed closely by females 21 years and older; males experienced the least overall cyberstalking with 33.5% of those under 21 being cyberstalking and 30% of those 21 and older being victimized.

Race

In terms of race, nonwhites experienced more overall cyberstalking victimization than did whites (48.8% compared to 39.8%); this difference is statistically significant: χ^2 (1, N = 964) = 3.24, p = 0.04. Across types of online victimization whites and nonwhites were victimized to a comparable degree, with the exception of unwanted contact. For this type of online pursuit behavior there is a statistically significant difference in victimization across race groups: χ^2 (1, N = 964) = 6.79, p = 0.008. None of the other differences in victimization across race groups are statistically significant for the other types of online pursuit behaviors or identity fraud victimization ($\alpha \leq 0.05$).

Table 5.2 also provides information related to the gender and race of cyberstalking victims. The group that experienced the most cyberstalking victimization was nonwhite females, with 53.2% of this group experiencing some form of cyberstalking during their lives. The next most frequently victimized group was white females with 45.4% of white women experiencing cyberstalking. Nonwhite males were the next most victimized group at 40%, followed by white men at 31%.

Table 5.1: Extent of Victimization by Demographics and Type of Online Victimization[a]

Type of Victimization

Demographic Characteristic	Contact % (n)	Harass % (n)	Sexual Advances % (n)	Threats Violence % (n)	ID Fraud % (n)	Cyberstalking % (n)
Sex (n)						
Males (379)	16.1% (61)	12.9% (49)	7.5% (28)	5.4% (20)	10.6% (39)	32.1% (122)
Females (593)	27.9% (165)**	25.2% (147)**	18.0% (104)**	3.7% (21)	10.6% (61)	46.3% (274)**
Age (n)						
Under 21 (591)	24.5% (145)	20.6% (121)	15.0% (87)	3.8% (22)	9.6% (55)	42.1% (249)
21 and Over	21.4% (82)	19.8% (75)	12.0% (45)	5.1% (19)	12.1% (45)	38.6% (148)
Race (n)						
White (828)	22.1% (168)	20.2% (169)	13.8% (114)	4.5% (37)	10.8% (88)	39.8% (335)
Nonwhite (135)	32.8% (40)**	21.8% (26)	14.5% (17)	3.5% (4)	10.1% (12)	48.8% (59)*
Rel. Status (n)						
Single (411)	18.8% (78)	19.3% (80)	11.1% (45)	4.0% (16)	10.5% (43)	36.8% (153)
Non-Single (558)	26.9% (149)**	21.1% (115)	16.1% (87)*	4.7% (25)	10.2% (57)	43.9% (243)**

*p ≤ 0.05; **p ≤ 0.01
[a] Numbers may not add to 974 due to missing data

Table 5.2: Percentage and Number of Males and Females Victimized[a] in Lifetime by Select Demographic Characteristics

Sex	Age		Race		Relationship Status	
	Under 21	21 and Over	White	Nonwhite	Single	Non-Single
Males	33.5% (77)	30.0% (45)	31.0% (102)	40.0% (18)	30.7% (65)	33.9% (65)
Females	47.8% (172)	44.0% (102)	45.4% (233)	53.2% (41)	43.1% (87)	48.2% (187)

[a]Based on summary cyberstalking measure.

Relationship Status
In Table 5.1 relationship status is presented as single and non-single (including dating, in a long-term relationship, married, and living with someone). The pattern that emerges from viewing the data this way is that non-singles are victimized more often than are people who are single. This was the case for every type of pursuit and the cyberstalking composite measure. For the overall cyberstalking variable, nearly 44% of those in a relationship have been cyberstalked as compared to 36.8% of those who are single, and this difference is statistically significant: χ^2 (1, N = 969) = 5.04, p = 0.01. There is also a statistically significant difference between singles and non-singles for harassment [(χ^2 (1, N = 959) = 8.88, p = 0.002] and sexual advances [(χ^2 (1, N = 948) = 4.89, p = 0.02]. The exception to this pattern is identity fraud victimization; slightly more singles in the sample experienced this form of victimization compared to non-singles (10.5% compared to 10.2%); this difference between singles and non-singles is not statistically significant [(χ^2 (1, N = 939) = 0.00, p = 0.54].

In examining relationship status and sex in combination, females are more likely to be cyberstalked than are males, regardless of relationship status. Among females, 48.2% of non-singles were victimized, and over 43% of singles were victims of cyberstalking. Single males experienced less victimization, with 30.7% males being victims of cyberstalking; nearly 34% of non-single males experienced some type of cyberstalking victimization.

Summary
A number of points warrant discussion regarding the estimates of cyberstalking victimization produced in the current study. First, it appears that cyberstalking victimization may be more prevalent than physically proximal stalking. If the estimates of lifetime prevalence are compared to the lifetime stalking estimates reported by Tjaden and Thoennes (1998) (i.e., 8% of women and 2% of men), they indicate that cyberstalking is more widespread than physical stalking. Second, compared to the estimates of cyberstalking victimization from previous self-report studies, the estimates produced in the current study suggest that this type of victimization is more prevalent than previously reported with nearly 41% of respondents being victimized at some time in their lives. Estimates of victimization from past work range between 3.7% (Alexy et al., 2005) and 31% (Spitzberg & Hoobler, 2002), mak-

ing the estimates from the current study the highest produced to date on the extent of cyberstalking victimization. One possible explanation for this figure is that multiple types of pursuit were included in the calculation of the overall cyberstalking victimization measure. Third, females are disproportionately victims of cyberstalking compared to males. This is true of every type of cyberstalking victimization with the exception of threats of violence. Fourth, beyond gender, certain groups appear to be disproportionately victimized. For instance, 53.2% of nonwhite females were victimized compared to 40% of nonwhite males. Further, single individuals were victimized less than those in relationships, which may indicate that dating partners are responsible for some portion of the stalking. Thus, to answer the first research question, the lifetime prevalence of cyberstalking victimization for members of the sample is nearly 41%, with different groups disproportionately being victimized. However, identifying which demographic groups have been victimized does not entirely explain what influences one's likelihood of victimization. To understand what exposes individuals to risk it is important to consider online lifestyles and routine activities within the domain of cyberstalking victimization.

BIVARIATE RESULTS

The bivariate relationships between the independent (and control) variables used in the study appear in Table 5.3. Point biserial correlation coefficients (r_{pb}) and Phi coefficients (φ) are used to assess the direction and strength of the association between two discrete variables. While these statistics describe the association between two variables, they do not take into account the effects of the other variables used in the analyses. The purpose of calculating such statistics is to gain an initial understanding of the general bivariate relationships between variables. The coefficients express both the direction and strength of a relationship and range between -1.00 and 1.00. While there is no universally agreed upon criteria for determining what constitutes a "strong" or "weak" relationship between two variables in the social sciences, Fox, Levin and Forde (2009) have provided the following general criteria: -1.00 (perfect negative correlation), -.60 (strong negative association), -.30 (moderate negative correlation), -.10 (weak negative correlation), .00 (no correlation), +.10 (weak positive correlation), +.30 (moderate positive correlation), +.60 (strong positive correlation), and 1.00 (perfect positive correlation). Table 5.4 illustrates the associations between the independent and dependent variables. Those bivariate relationships in Table 4.4 that are weak[26] or better according to the Fox et al. criteria and statistically significant ($\alpha \leq 0.05$) will be discussed below.

Online Exposure

As reported in Table 5.4, each of the online exposure variables is statistically associated with having experienced cyberstalking victimization. Specifically, the amount of time spent online is positively associated with unwanted contact ($r_{pb} = .075$, $p \leq .05$) and threats of violence ($r_{pb} = .075$, $p \leq .05$). The number of online social networks owned by the respondent is positively related to all six types of online victimization, but has the strongest relationship with overall cyberstalking ($r_{pb} = .210$, $p \leq .001$). Likewise, the number of times a day an individual updates their online social networking website is positively related to five of the six dependent variables, with the sole exception being online threats. The number of hours per day spent engaging in online networking is positively associated with three types of cyberstalking—namely, unwanted contact ($r_{pb} = .101$, $p \leq .01$), sexual advances ($r_{pb} = .082$, $p \leq .05$), and overall cyberstalking ($r_{pb} = .105$, $p \leq .001$). Further, the number of photos posted on one's online social network is positively associated with all of the victimization variables except threats of violence, and the use of AOL Instant Messenger is significantly and positively associated with each of the following: unwanted contact ($\varphi = .088$, $p \leq .01$); harassment ($\varphi = .068$, $p \leq .05$); sexual advances ($\varphi = .079$, $p \leq .05$); and the summary cyberstalking measure ($\varphi = .155$, $p \leq .001$). While these relationships can all be characterized as weak, they nevertheless suggest that to some degree online exposure puts one at risk for cyberstalking victimization.

---

[26] Weak or better relationships are reported because none of the relationships are moderately strong or better.

Table 5.3: Bivariate Relationships[a] between Independent Variables and Control Variables

Variable	1	2	3	4	5	6	7	8	9	10
(1) Time Online	1.00									
(2) Number SN	.187**	1.00								
(3) SN Updates	.200**	.120**	1.00							
(4) Time on SN	.496**	.242**	.366**	1.00						
(5) Photos on SN	-.032	.042	.083**	.110**	1.00					
(6) AOL IM	.205**	.235**	.112**	.197**	.061	1.00				
(7) SN Private	-.022	-.061	-.021	.014	.150**	.001	1.00			
(8) Profile Tracker	.109**	.273**	.044	.201**	.073*	.096**	.000	1.00		
(9) Add Stranger	.047	.132**	.084**	.104**	.037	.044	-.037	.079*	1.00	
(10) Friends on SN	.064*	.189**	.066*	.195**	.276**	.099**	.025	.111**	.168**	1.00
(11) Friend Service	.036	.112**	.062	.101**	.000	.007	-.023	.060	.064*	.112**
(12) Attractiveness	.071*	.169**	.244**	.153**	.202**	.246**	-.023	.183**	.154**	.187**
(13) Deviance	.069*	.203**	.054	.108**	.073*	.112**	-.075*	.118**	.146**	.119**
(14) Low Self-Cont.	.030	.081*	.071*	.030	.046	.067*	-.011	.111**	.090**	.093**
(15) Gender	-.089**	.056	-.010	.102**	.255**	.020	.177**	.135**	-.070*	.038
(16) Age	.005	.067*	-.121**	-.086**	.052	-.027	.008	.055	-.011	-.058
(17) Nonwhite	.140**	.055	.033	.130**	-.084**	-.075*	-.028	.090**	.016	.067*
(18) Non-single	-.055	.064*	.002	.021	.107**	.038	.090**	.067*	-.015	.027
(19) Peer Deviance	.027	.093**	.102**	.046	.052	.097**	.038	.074*	.115**	.090**
(20) Offline Risk	.003	-.072*	.012	-.002	.178**	.001	.058	-.004	.151**	.209**

[a] Due to differences in level of measurement across variables, three types of correlation coefficients are reported – Pearson's r, point biserial correlation coefficients (r_{pb}) and Phi coefficients (φ). * $p \leq 0.05$; ** $p \leq 0.01$.

Table 5.3 (Continued): Bivariate Relationships[a] between Independent Variables and Control Variables

Variable	11	12	13	14	15	16	17	18	19	20
(1) Time Online										
(2) Number SN										
(3) SN Updates										
(4) Time on SN										
(5) Photos on SN										
(6) AOL IM										
(7) SN Private										
(8) Profile Tracker										
(9) Add Stranger										
(10) Friends on SN										
(11) Friend Service	1.00									
(12) Attractiveness	-.014	1.00								
(13) Deviance	.078*	.078*	1.00							
(14) Low Self-Cont.	.089**	.043	.115**	1.00						
(15) Gender	-.002	-.039	-.040	-.078*	1.00					
(16) Age	.045	-.039	.063*	.010	.013	1.00				
(17) Nonwhite	.122**	-.078*	.128**	.015	.015	.010	1.00			
(18) Non-single	.027	.013	.038	.111**	.217**	.090**	-.056	1.00		
(19) Peer Deviance	.103**	.120**	.140**	.128**	.001	.018	-.024	.012	1.00	
(20) Offline Risk	-.004	.077*	.184**	.132**	-.115**	.096**	-.096**	.005	.138**	1.00

[a] Due to differences in level of measurement across variables, three types of correlation coefficients are reported – Pearson's r, point biserial correlation coefficients (r_{pb}) and Phi coefficients (φ). * $p \leq 0.05$; ** $p \leq 0.01$.

Table 5.4: Bivariate Relationships[a] between Independent/Control Variables and Victimization Variables

Independent Variables	Contact	Harass	Sexual Advances	Threats Violence	Cyberstalking	ID Fraud
Exposure						
Time Online	.075*	.019	.021	.075*	.048	-.008
# SN	.176***	.129***	.157***	.087**	.210***	.071*
# Updates	.065*	.080*	.122***	-.008	.126***	.109***
Time on SN	.101**	.047	.082*	.042	.105***	.051
# Photos SN	.085**	.065*	.092**	-.034	.136***	.095**
AOL IM	.088**	.068*	.079*	.053	.155***	.037
Guardianship						
SN Private	.039	.023	.031	.004	.045	.006
Profile Track	.184***	.071*	.140***	.120***	.183***	.084**

* p ≤ 0.05; ** p ≤ 0.01; *** p ≤ 0.001
[a] Due to differences in level of measurement across variables, two types of correlation coefficients are reported – point biserial correlation coefficients (r_{pb}) and Phi coefficients (φ).

Table 5.4 (Continued): Bivariate Relationships[a] between Independent/Control Variables and Victimization Variables

Independent Variables	Contact	Harass	Sexual Advances	Threats Violence	Cyberstalking	ID Fraud
Proximity						
Add Stranger	.153***	.142***	.147***	.041	.218***	.131***
# Friends SN	.104***	.048	.116***	-.024	.121***	.092**
Friend Service	.063*	.028	.083*	.030	.072*	.113***
Target Att.	.084**	.078*	.084**	.005	.135***	.041
Deviance	.182***	.163***	.208***	.116***	.240***	.098**
LSC Controls	.149***	.053	.063*	.070*	.110***	.094**
Gender	.137***	.149***	.149***	-.041	.141***	.061
Age	-.017	-.040	.046	.005	-.005	-.060
Nonwhite	.084**	.013	.006	-.017	.057	-.005
Non-Single	.096**	.021	.072*	.018	.072*	.078*
Peer Deviance	.181***	.173***	.191***	.083**	.226***	.157***
Offline Risk	.009	-.035	.064*	.024	.035	.090**

* $p \leq 0.05$; ** $p \leq 0.01$; *** $p \leq 0.001$

Online Guardianship

Of the two online guardianship variables, only use of a profile tracker is significantly related to victimization. According to Table 5.4, the use of profile trackers on online social networks is positively related to all six types of victimization as follows: unwanted contact ($\varphi = .184$, $p \leq .001$); harassment ($\varphi = .071$, $p \leq .05$); sexual advances ($\varphi = .140$, $p \leq .001$); threats of violence ($\varphi = .120$, $p \leq .001$); overall cyberstalking ($\varphi = .183$, $p \leq .001$); and identity fraud victimization ($\varphi = .084$, $p \leq .01$). These results suggest that online guardianship, as operationalized in the current study, does not protect individuals from online victimization. Indeed, while using a profile tracker is significantly related to victimization, the effects are the opposite of expectations. This may reflect a temporal ordering issue, where respondents acquired online tracking programs after experiencing cyberstalking or other comparable problems online. It may also be that these theoretical concepts are not necessarily mutually exclusive. For instance, the *add stranger* variable will be discussed below in terms of online proximity because adding strangers as friends to online profiles brings potentially motivated offenders into online proximity with potential targets. However, not adding strangers as friends could also be considered a form of self-guardianship, so it may not be the case that guardianship has no effect on victimization but rather that neither of these two variables produced the expected protective results.

Online Proximity

As the results in Table 5.4 illustrate, all three of the online proximity variables have consistent effects across types of online pursuit. For instance, the *add stranger* variable (measuring whether the respondent allows strangers access to their online social networks) is significantly and positively associated with all of the types of online victimization with the exception of online threats. These variable effects are as follows: unwanted contact ($\varphi = .153$, $p \leq .001$); harassment ($\varphi = .142$, $p \leq .001$); sexual advances ($\varphi = .147$, $p \leq .001$); overall cyberstalking ($\varphi = .218$, $p \leq .001$); and identity fraud victimization ($\varphi = .131$, $p \leq .001$). The number of friends a respondent has online and the use of a friend service are positively related to four of the six types of victimization—namely, contact, sexual advances, ID fraud and overall cyberstalking; the magnitude of these effects are presented in Table 5.4. Once again, while these relationships are considered weak, they do point to the potential importance of online proximity to motivated offenders in explaining the occurrence of cyberstalking victimization.

Online Target Attractiveness
As can be seen in Table 5.4, online target attractiveness is significantly and positively associated with each of the following: unwanted contact (r_{pb} = .084, $p \leq .01$); harassment (r_{pb} = .078, $p \leq .05$); sexual advances (r_{pb} = .084, $p \leq .01$); and the summary cyberstalking measure (r_{pb} = .135, $p \leq .001$). This relationship is relatively weak, but this evidence is encouraging in terms of the applicability of the theoretical concept in explaining online types of victimization.

Online Deviance
Table 5.4 indicates that participating in online deviance is positively and statistically associated with all six of the online victimization measures: contact (r_{pb} = .182, $p \leq .001$); harassment (r_{pb} = .163, $p \leq .001$); sexual advances (r_{pb} = .208, $p \leq .001$); threats (r_{pb} = .116, $p \leq .001$); overall cyberstalking (r_{pb} = .240, $p \leq .001$), and identity fraud victimization (r_{pb} = .098, $p \leq .01$). These findings provide preliminary support for the idea that a deviant online lifestyle (e.g., hacking, media piracy, harassment) puts one at added risk of online victimization.

Low Self-Control
As argued above, a propensity toward low self-control might increase one's likelihood of online victimization by agitating/aggravating others online into retaliation (e.g., threats), or by making one more likely to give out information or participate in risky online encounters. As the results reported in Table 5.4 indicate, the low self-control measure is positively and statistically associated with each of the following: contact (r_{pb} = .149, $p \leq .001$); sexual advances (r_{pb} = .063, $p \leq .05$); online threats (r_{pb} = .070, $p \leq .05$); overall cyberstalking (r_{pb} = .110, $p \leq .001$); and identity fraud (r_{pb} = .094, $p \leq .01$).

Summary
Overall, the bivariate results indicate that the lifestyle-routine activities perspective may have some utility in explaining cyberstalking victimization. Each of the lifestyle-routine activities theory (LRAT) concepts of online exposure, online proximity, online target attractiveness, online deviance and low self-control produced significant bivariate relationships ($\alpha \leq 0.05$). In particular, online exposure and online deviance were consistently related to victimization across the several types of online pursuit and identity fraud victimization; these two relationships are statistically significant at the $\alpha \leq 0.05$ level. The bivariate results also suggest possible risk factors for cyberstalking victimization (e.g., spending more time online, granting strangers access to personal information, engaging in deviant routine activities online). To more fully explore the effects of the LRAT variables on victimization, binary logistic regression models will be presented below.

MULTIVARIATE RESULTS

Before modeling the relationships between online lifestyles/routines and stalking cybervictimization, it is necessary to check for multicollinearity among the independent variables. Multicollinearity occurs when predictor variables in a multiple regression are highly correlated, and makes it difficult to determine the relative contributions of such variables to the variation in the dependent variable. Accordingly, tolerance and variance inflation factor statistics were calculated to determine whether multicollinearity exists between the various study variables. As illustrated in Appendix 8, multicollinearity is not a statistical issue with the variables used in this analysis.

Missing data, however, pose a potential problem in the following analysis. A substantial number of missing cases may call into question the validity of the results. For this reason, missing values on the independent variables were imputed using maximum likelihood (ML) estimation techniques[27]. This technique uses the expectation maximization (EM) algorithm and a two-step estimation process (i.e., an expectation step and a maximization step) to substitute ML estimates for cases with

---

[27] As noted previously, it is not advisable to impute missing data on dependent variables, which is why only missing values on the independent variables were imputed using maximum likelihood estimation (Allison, 2001).

missing values. As Allison (2001: 19) has explained, "These two steps are repeated multiple times in an iterative process that eventually converges to the ML estimates." This technique has been described as efficient, practical, and especially effective for large samples; it is considered superior to imputation by multiple regression techniques because it makes fewer demands on the level of measurement of the data (Allison, 2001; Garson, 2006). The maximum likelihood technique is also currently the most common method of missing data imputation (Garson, 2006). Binary logistic regression models were estimated both on the imputed data and the original data (with missing values). The results were not substantively different across analyses, so only the models featuring the imputed data will be presented and discussed below.

Tables 5.5 through 5.10 provide logistic regression coefficients, standard errors, and odds ratios for the four types of online pursuit, for identity fraud, and for the overall cyberstalking victimization variable. The regression coefficients represent log odds, meaning that for every one unit change in the independent variable there is a change in the log of the odds (corresponding to the value of the coefficient). If the log of the odds is positive, the probability of the outcome increases as the value of the variable increases; if the log of the odds is negative, the probability of the outcome decreases as the value of the variable increases. Since the interpretation of the coefficient values is not intuitive, odds ratios (exponentiated coefficients) are also presented. For Exp(B), values greater than 1.00 mean that odds increase as the independent variable increases, while values less than 1.00 mean odds decrease as the independent variable increases. As an example, a value of 2.27 (the log odds of online deviance on online harassment) is difficult to interpret, but an odds ratio of 9.72 (for engaging in online deviance) can be interpreted as an increase in online harassment by 9.7 times as participation in online deviance increases.

Model fit statistics, including -2 log likelihood (-2LL), model chi-square (G_M), and Nagelkerke R^2 are also presented in Tables 5.5 through 5.10. The -2 log likelihood represents an index of the model's fit, with the value of the statistic being higher in poorly fitting statistical models. The value of the statistic is reduced as explanatory variables are added to the model improving the model's fit, with a perfectly fitting model having a -2 log likelihood value of zero (Mertler & Vannatta, 2005). This reduction indicates that the model is better at predicting the dependent variable than it was before the addition of the independent variable(s).

To measure how much improved the model is as independent variables are added, the model chi-square statistic is calculated (Field, 2005). This statistic represents the difference between a model containing only the constant and the particular model under examination (Mertler & Vannatta, 2005). According to Menard (2002, 2010), if the value of G_M is statistically significant, the null hypothesis is rejected and it can be concluded that the inclusion of the independent variables in the model improves prediction of the dependent variable over a model in which only the constant is present. The Nagelkerke R^2 statistic also offers a measure of the significance of the model. The value of this statistic represents the proportion of variation in the dependent variable that is explained by the independent variables. For instance, in Model 1 (Table 5.5) the independent variables explain 20% of the variation in unwanted contact victimization (Nagelkerke $R^2 = 0.20$). Overall then, the model fit statistics for Models 1-6 presented in the tables indicate that these models fit well with the data. The results of the logistic regression analyses for each of these six dependent variables will be presented and discussed below in Tables 5.5 through 5.10.

Online Exposure

As Tables 5.5 through 5.10 illustrate, the online exposure variables are not consistent predictors of cyberstalking and identity fraud victimization across statistical models. There are, however, a few variables that yielded statistically significant effects on victimization. For instance, the online exposure variable measuring the number of times a day the respondent updates their online social networking account (SN Update) is a statistically significant and positive predictor of receiving unwanted sexual advances. The magnitude of this effect is quite modest however, as is also the case for identity fraud victimization. The number of social networking accounts that a respondent has opened (Number SN) is also a positive predictor of victimization, increasing the odds of unwanted contact and overall cyberstalking victimization slightly. The final online exposure variable to produce statistically significant effects is the variable measuring whether the respondent uses AOL Instant Messenger (IM). Use of AOL IM increases odds of overall cyberstalking victimization by nearly 1.5 times. None of the other online exposure variables produced statistically significant effects on any of the six victimization variables.

Online Guardianship
For the concept of online guardianship, use of a profile tracker by the respondent increases odds of victimization for four of the six types of online victimization. As Tables 5.5, 5.7, 5.8, and 5.9 indicate, for unwanted contact, sexual advances, and overall cyberstalking victimization, odds of victimization are nearly doubled by use of an online profile tracker, and for online threats of violence odds of victimization are nearly tripled. These findings are contrary to expectations, since these programs are designed to permit users to keep track of who is viewing their information and enable them to take measures to limit access of potential offenders if problems develop. One explanation for this counterintuitive finding is that the effect may reflect a reactive response to victimization rather than serve as a precursor to it. Individuals who experienced problems with cybervictimization may have adopted profile trackers to stay safe in the future.

Online Proximity
As the findings reported in Tables 5.5 through 5.10 indicate, the online proximity variables are among the strongest and most robust predictors of victimization across types of cyberstalking. In particular, the *add stranger* variable, indicating whether the respondent allows people they do not know access to their personal profile pages (e.g., social networks) online, increases risks of victimization for five of the six dependent variables. For unwanted contact and harassment, adding a stranger increases odds of victimization by more than two times; for sexual advances and overall cyberstalking, doing so increases odds of victimization over 2.5 times; and for identity fraud, adding a stranger increases odds of victimization by nearly three times. The second statistically significant predictor of victimization is use of a friend service. These services (e.g., friend trains, whore trains) allow the host (the website) to "advertise" the user's profile, and automatically bring the

user into contact with other users who are looking for online friends (or for something more). Individuals who used these services are more likely to experience identity fraud, suggesting that offenders may seek opportunities for victimization through these services. Use of a friend service increases odds of identity fraud victimization nearly 2.7 times.

Table 5.5: Binary Logistic Regression Coefficients, Standard Errors, and Exponentiated Coefficients for Unwanted Contact

Variables	Coefficient	S.E.	Exp(B)
Model 1: Unwanted Contact			
Exposure			
Time Online	0.05	(0.04)	1.05
Number SN	0.10*	(0.05)	1.11
SN Updates	0.00	(0.02)	1.00
Time on SN	-0.04	(0.06)	0.96
Photos on SN	0.00	(0.00)	1.00
AOL IM	0.07	(0.18)	1.08
Guardianship			
SN Private	0.29	(0.24)	1.34
Profile Tracker	0.60*	(0.24)	1.83
Proximity			
Add Stranger	0.75***	(0.22)	2.12
Friends on SN	0.00	(0.00)	1.00
Friend Service	0.05	(0.42)	1.05
T. Attractiveness	0.15	(0.41)	1.16
Deviance	1.86***	(0.54)	6.42
Low Self-Control	0.49**	(0.16)	1.63
Controls			
Gender	0.70***	(0.20)	2.02
Age	-0.26	(0.18)	0.77
Nonwhite	0.40	(0.25)	1.49
Non-single	0.29	(0.18)	1.33
Deviant Peers	0.19***	(0.05)	1.21
Risky Offline Act.	-0.01	(0.01)	0.99
Constant	-5.12***	(0.57)	0.01
-2 Log-likelihood	921.44		
Model χ^2	136.22***		
Nagelkerke R^2	0.20		
N	974		

* $p \leq .05$; ** $p \leq .01$; *** $p \leq .001$

Table 5.6: Binary Logistic Regression Coefficients, Standard Errors, and Exponentiated Coefficients for Online Harassment

Model 2: Harassment

Variables	Coefficient	S.E.	Exp(B)
Exposure			
Time Online	0.02	(0.04)	1.02
Number SN	0.08	(0.06)	1.09
SN Updates	0.03	(0.02)	1.03
Time on SN	-0.08	(0.07)	0.92
Photos on SN	0.00	(0.00)	1.00
AOL IM	0.03	(0.19)	1.03
Guardianship			
SN Private	0.15	(0.24)	1.16
Profile Tracker	0.03	(0.27)	1.03
Proximity			
Add Stranger	0.83***	(0.23)	2.28
Friends on SN	0.00	(0.00)	1.00
Friend Service	-0.02	(0.45)	0.98
T. Attractiveness	0.34	(0.43)	1.40
Deviance	2.27***	(0.56)	9.72
Low Self-Control	0.14	(0.17)	1.15
Controls			
Gender	0.95***	(0.21)	2.59
Age	-0.28	(0.19)	0.75
Nonwhite	-0.10	(0.27)	0.90
Non-single	-0.11	(0.18)	0.90
Deviant Peers	0.20***	(0.05)	1.22
Risky Offline Act.	-0.02*	(0.01)	0.98
Constant	-4.07***	(0.57)	0.02
-2 Log-likelihood	871.21		
Model χ^2	102.37***		
Nagelkerke R^2	0.16		
N	964		

* $p \leq .05$; ** $p \leq .01$; *** $p \leq .001$

Table 5.7: Binary Logistic Regression Coefficients, Standard Errors, and Exponentiated Coefficients for Sexual Advances

Model 3: Sexual Advances

Variables	Coefficient	S.E.	Exp(B)
Exposure			
Time Online	-0.02	(0.05)	0.99
Number SN	0.08	(0.06)	1.08
SN Updates	0.07**	(0.02)	1.07
Time on SN	-0.07	(0.08)	0.94
Photos on SN	0.00	(0.00)	1.00
AOL IM	0.09	(0.23)	1.09
Guardianship			
SN Private	0.16	(0.30)	1.18
Profile Tracker	0.57*	(0.29)	1.77
Proximity			
Add Stranger	0.93**	(0.30)	2.53
Friends on SN	0.00	(0.00)	1.00
Friend Service	0.47	(0.47)	1.60
T. Attractiveness	0.15	(0.52)	1.17
Deviance	2.88***	(0.64)	17.81
Low Self-Control	-0.04	(0.20)	0.96
Controls			
Gender	1.22***	(0.27)	3.37
Age	0.18	(0.22)	1.20
Nonwhite	-0.26	(0.33)	0.77
Non-single	0.18	(0.22)	1.20
Deviant Peers	0.21***	(0.06)	1.23
Risky Offline Act.	0.01	(0.01)	1.01
Constant	-5.37***	(0.70)	0.01
-2 Log-likelihood	641.39		
Model χ^2	125.29***		
Nagelkerke R^2	0.22		
N	953		

* $p \leq .05$; ** $p \leq .01$; *** $p \leq .001$

Table 5.8: Binary Logistic Regression Coefficients, Standard Errors, and Exponentiated Coefficients for Threats of Violence

Model 4: Threats of Violence

Variables	Coefficient	S.E.	Exp(B)
Exposure			
Time Online	0.09	(0.06)	1.09
Number SN	0.07	(0.09)	1.07
SN Updates	-0.04	(0.05)	0.96
Time on SN	-0.02	(0.11)	0.98
Photos on SN	0.00	(0.00)	1.00
AOL IM	0.12	(0.38)	1.13
Guardianship			
SN Private	0.46	(0.49)	1.59
Profile Tracker	1.10*	(0.44)	2.99
Proximity			
Add Stranger	0.20	(0.44)	1.23
Friends on SN	-0.00	(0.00)	0.99
Friend Service	0.39	(0.77)	1.48
T. Attractiveness	-0.44	(0.76)	0.64
Deviance	2.41*	(0.99)	11.13
Low Self-Control	0.40	(0.32)	1.50
Controls			
Gender	-0.38	(0.38)	0.68
Age	-0.23	(0.36)	0.79
Nonwhite	-0.68	(0.60)	0.50
Non-single	0.09	(0.36)	1.10
Deviant Peers	0.13	(0.09)	1.14
Risky Offline Act.	0.01	(0.01)	1.00
Constant	-5.26***	(1.05)	0.01
-2 Log-likelihood	302.09		
Model χ^2	35.12*		
Nagelkerke R^2	0.12		
N	942		

* $p \leq .05$; ** $p \leq .01$; *** $p \leq .001$

Table 5.9: Binary Logistic Regression Coefficients, Standard Errors, and Exponentiated Coefficients for Overall Cyberstalking Victimization

Variables	Coefficient	S.E.	Exp(B)
Model 5: Cyberstalking			
Exposure			
Time Online	-0.00	(0.03)	0.99
Number SN	0.13**	(0.05)	1.14
SN Updates	0.04	(0.02)	1.04
Time on SN	-0.06	(0.05)	0.94
Photos on SN	0.00	(0.00)	1.00
AOL IM	0.38*	(0.16)	1.46
Guardianship			
SN Private	0.28	(0.21)	1.32
Profile Tracker	0.59*	(0.24)	1.80
Proximity			
Add Stranger	0.93***	(0.18)	2.53
Friends on SN	0.00	(0.00)	1.00
Friend Service	0.12	(0.43)	1.13
T. Attractiveness	0.19	(0.35)	1.21
Deviance	2.59***	(0.52)	13.29
Low Self-Control	0.19	(0.15)	1.21
Controls			
Gender	0.62***	(0.17)	1.85
Age	-0.13	(0.16)	0.88
Nonwhite	0.27	(0.23)	1.32
Non-single	0.09	(0.15)	1.09
Deviant Peers	0.25***	(0.05)	1.28
Risky Offline Act.	-0.01	(0.01)	0.99
Constant	-3.85***	(0.49)	0.02
-2 Log-likelihood	1111.82		
Model χ^2	204.97 ***		
Nagelkerke R^2	0.26		
N	974		

* $p \leq .05$; ** $p \leq .01$; *** $p \leq .001$

Table 5.10: Binary Logistic Regression Coefficients, Standard Errors, and Exponentiated Coefficients for Identity Fraud

Model 6: Identity Fraud

Variables	Coefficient	S.E.	Exp(B)
Exposure			
Time Online	-0.04	(0.06)	0.96
Number SN	0.05	(0.07)	1.05
SN Updates	0.05*	(0.03)	1.06
Time on SN	-0.03	(0.08)	0.98
Photos on SN	0.00	(0.00)	1.00
AOL IM	0.05	(0.25)	1.05
Guardianship			
SN Private	-0.06	(0.31)	0.95
Profile Tracker	0.51	(0.32)	1.67
Proximity			
Add Stranger	1.02**	(0.35)	2.78
Friends on SN	0.00	(0.00)	1.00
Friend Service	0.98*	(0.46)	2.66
T. Attractiveness	-0.62	(0.56)	0.54
Deviance	0.85	(0.74)	2.34
Low Self-Control	0.22	(0.22)	1.24
Controls			
Gender	0.40	(0.27)	1.49
Age	-0.67**	(0.26)	0.51
Nonwhite	-0.22	(0.37)	0.80
Non-single	0.43	(0.24)	1.53
Deviant Peers	0.18**	(0.06)	1.20
Risky Offline Act.	0.02	(0.01)	1.02
Constant	-4.48***	(0.74)	0.01
-2 Log-likelihood	564.40		
Model χ^2	73.37***		
Nagelkerke R^2	0.15		
N	943		

* $p \leq .05$; ** $p \leq .01$; *** $p \leq .001$

Online Target Attractiveness

The online target attractiveness measure, which was comprised of nine separate indicators of target attractiveness, is not significantly associated with any of the cyberstalking victimization dependent variables or identity fraud victimization. This is contrary to expectations that a more attractive target is more likely to be targeted by motivated offenders. It was hypothesized that individuals who provide more personally identifying information and/or information making it easier for cyberstalkers to contact victims would present more attractive targets. However, it is possible that the current measure of target attractiveness is not a reliable measure of the LRAT concept.

Online Deviance

As reported in Tables 5.5 through 5.9, online deviance is the strongest predictor of victimization in five of the six logistic regression models, increasing odds of unwanted contact over six times, harassment nearly ten times, sexual advances nearly 18 times, threats of violence over 11 times, and overall cyberstalking over 13 times. As discussed in Chapter 2, participation in deviant lifestyles is hypothesized to have the effect of exposing these individuals to added risks of victimization (e.g., they are likely to come into contact with others engaging in the same sorts of activities, they open themselves up to retaliation if they are caught or confronted). The measure of deviance utilized in the present study was based on measures of participation in eight deviant activities (e.g., hacking, sexting, online harassment, media piracy), and the strong relationships between this measure and the victimization variables indicates that engaging in these activities is not only illegal in many circumstances, but is also a precursor to cybervictimization.

Low Self-Control

With the exception of unwanted contact, low self-control failed to stand out as a predictor of cyberstalking victimization. For unwanted contact, individuals characterized as possessing low self-control are over 1.6 times more likely to be the recipients of unwanted contact (i.e., being contacted after asking the other person to cease communication). Individuals having low self-control may be more likely to participate in risky activities online (e.g., downloading illicit materials that may include viruses, being less careful in deciding to whom to allow access to their personal information online), or may behave in such ways as to pester or provoke others into contacting them in a retributive way. The statistically significant bivariate relationship between low self-control and online deviance ($r = 0.115$, $p \leq 0.001$) provides support for the former proposition.

Control Variables

Among the several control variables, gender stands out as a predictor of victimization for four of the five cyberstalking victimization variables. Specifically, being female is a positive predictor of unwanted contact, harassment, sexual advances, and overall cyberstalking. Age affects only one type of cybervictimization, with individuals over 21 years old being less likely to experience identity fraud victimization. The *deviant peers* control variable is a significant and positive predictor of five of the six dependent variables, increasing the odds of unwanted contact, harassment, sexual advances, overall cyberstalking and identity fraud. The final control variable to affect odds of victimization is participation in offline risky activities; however, such activities were negatively associated with harassment victimization, and the variable effects are rather modest.

SUMMARY

When examining the five cyberstalking victimization variables and the identity fraud victimization variable, several discernible patterns emerge. A summary of the effects of the lifestyle-routine activities variables on cyberstalking victimization and identity fraud victimization appear in Table 5.11. First, online exposure increases risks for unwanted contact, sexual advances, overall cyberstalking, and identity fraud victimization. Of the six measures of online exposure, three variables exhibited effects on cybervictimization—namely, use of AOL IM, the number of online social networks, and the number of daily updates to online social networks. Second, the indicators of online guardianship did not reduce victimization; in fact, use of an online profile tracker is a significant, positive predictor of victimization. Third, two of the online proximity variables are positively related to victimization. In particular, adding strangers as friends to online social networks had fairly robust effects across models, increasing the likelihood of victimization for five of the six types of cybervictimization. This is consistent with lifestyle-routine activities theory, as greater proximity to motivated offenders (whether in physical space or online) is expected to result in added risk of victimization. Fourth, online target attractiveness did not yield any statistically significant effects across types of cyberstalking or identity fraud. Theoretically, a more attractive target would be more likely to be targeted/pursued by offenders, but this was not the case in the current analysis. Fifth, online deviance is a robust predictor of cyberstalking victimization for every type of victimization except identity fraud, with those participating in online deviance being more likely to experience cyberstalking. Not only are the effects of online deviance consistent, but they are strong. For instance, as Table 5.7 illustrates, participating in online deviance increases the risk of being the recipient of unwanted sexual advances by nearly 18 times. Finally, consistent with Gottfredson and Hirschi's (1990) general theory of crime, individuals characterized as having low self-control are more likely to be cyberstalked; however, this was only the case for unwanted contact.

Chapter 6 concludes the study with a discussion of these results, particularly in terms of the extent of victimization, in terms of what puts individuals at risk, and with respect to the implications of the findings for lifestyle-routine activities theory. Suggestions for preventing cyberstalking will also be presented, followed by an assessment of the limitations of the study and possible directions for future cyberstalking victimization research.

Table 5.11: Summary of Lifestyle-Routine Activities Findings for Cyberstalking Victimization

Unwanted Contact	Harassment	Sexual Advances	Threats of Violence	Cyberstalking Victimization	Identity Fraud
Number of Social Networks (Exposure)	Add Stranger (Proximity)	Number of Social Network Updates (Exposure)		Number of Social Networks (Exposure)	Number of Social Network Updates (Exposure)
Profile Tracker (Exposure)		Profile Tracker (Guardianship)	Profile Tracker (Proximity)	AOL IM (Exposure) Profile Tracker (Guardianship)	
Add Stranger (Proximity)		Add Stranger (Proximity)		Add Stranger (Proximity)	Add Stranger (Proximity)
Online Deviance	Online Deviance	Online Deviance	Online Deviance	Online Deviance	Friend Service (Proximity)
LSC					

CHAPTER 6
Summary, Implications, and the Future of Cyberstalking Research

This final chapter will address each of the three research questions that have guided the study: (1) what is the extent of cyberstalking victimization amongst members of the sample?; (2) what puts college students at risk for cyberstalking victimization?; and (3) can lifestyle-routine activities theory be adapted to explain victimizations in cyberspace among this group of victims? Next, the implications of the study results for preventing cyberstalking in the future will be discussed, followed by a review of the limitations of the study, directions for future research, and some concluding remarks.

SUMMARY OF RESULTS

Extent of Victimization
The lifetime prevalence of overall cyberstalking amongst members of the sample of college students is 40.8%. Of those respondents who were cyberstalked, 23.3% experienced unwanted contact, 20.1% experienced harassment, 13.9% were the target of unwanted sexual advances, and 4.4% were threatened with violence. One in ten respondents experienced identity fraud victimization. These estimates raise three important points. First, if this finding were to be reaffirmed through replication, it would suggest that cyberstalking is more prevalent[28] than

---

[28] Estimates from Tjaden and Thoennes' (1998) national-level study of stalking estimate prevalence at 8.1% of women and 2.1% of men, and in assessments of

physically proximal stalking. Second, while only a speculative observation, cyberstalking may partially account for why there appears to have been a surge in stalking victimization over the last decade. In 1998, Tjaden and Thoeness reported that one million residents of the United States had experienced stalking in the 12 months prior to the survey. In 2009, Baum et al. (2009) published results of a national study on stalking indicating that 3.4 million adults in the United States had been stalked in the year before the survey was administered[29]. Cyberstalking may account for some of the disparity in these estimates, as technologies making cyberstalking victimization possible (e.g., proliferation of the Internet and Internet-capable devices) have spread exponentially during this time. Third, this estimate is higher than previously published estimates of cyberstalking victimization. As discussed in Chapter 1, current estimates of cyberstalking victimization range[30] widely from 3.5% to over 31% of sample populations (Spitzberg & Hoobler, 2002). One of the reasons for this diversity in estimates is that most studies of cyberstalking victimization to date have only reported estimates of the harassment element of cyberstalking, neglecting the other types of pursuit behaviors that comprise this type of victimization (i.e., unwanted contact, sexual advances, threats of violence).

In addition to estimating the extent of cyberstalking victimization, the current study also identified groups that are most at risk of victimization. It was hypothesized that those possessing certain demographic characteristics (e.g., being female) would be disproportionately victimized, and the data collected in this study supported this expectation. For instance, females were significantly more likely to be the victims of unwanted contact, online harassment, sexual advances, and overall

---

the extant literature, Sheridan, Blaauw, and Davies (2003) reported that estimates from studies of the lifetime prevalence of stalking range from 12% to 16% for women and 4% to 7% for men, while Spitzberg and Cupach (2007) reported ranges of 8% to 32% for women and 2% to 13% for men in their assessment.

[29] Measurement of stalking across these two studies is fairly comparable, although Tjaden and Thoennes (1998) did not measure cyberstalking victimization, while Baum et al. (2009) did.

[30] This range does not include Bocij's (2003) study estimate of 82%.

cyberstalking than were males; nonwhites experienced more unwanted contact and overall cyberstalking than did whites; and regarding relationship status, non-singles were significantly more likely to be victims of unwanted contact, sexual advances, and overall cyberstalking than were single individuals. Moving beyond demographic explanations of victimization, the current study also identified those lifestyles and routine activities that put individuals at greater risk for cyberstalking victimization.

Lifestyles and Routine Activities as Risk Factors for Cyberstalking
The second research question asked what factors put individuals at risk of cyberstalking victimization[31]. It was hypothesized that online lifestyles and routine activities may make some individuals more likely to be victimized. The logistic regression results indicate that this is the case, with a number of online activities increasing victimization risk.

Online Exposure
As discussed in Chapter 4, the LRAT concept of exposure is hypothesized to increase victimization by increasing individuals' exposure to motivated offenders and risky situations (Cohen et al., 1981). In the current analysis, three measures of online exposure are associated with increases in cyberstalking victimization: (1) the number of social networks the respondent has opened; (2) the number of daily updates to those networks; and, (3) the use of AOL Instant Messenger. The victim's number of social networks and the number of daily updates to these networks theoretically both provide more opportunities for victimization. For instance, someone who provides information and daily updates on multiple online social networks reaches a larger "audience" than someone who only maintains and updates a single online network account. The third exposure variable to produce statistically significant results with victimization is use of AOL Instant Messenger. AOL IM is a real time communication application used with computers or wire-

---

[31] This measure includes the four types of pursuit, and does not include identity fraud victimization.

less devices (e.g., iPhone) that allows users to send text back and forth. The ease and immediacy of communication allowed by AOL IM makes various pursuit behaviors a relatively simple task for cyberstalkers. Further, AOL IM does not require users to obtain permission before adding other users to their buddy lists. In essence, not only are stalkers able to easily communicate with their victims in real time, but they can also monitor whether their victims are online or not, which can facilitate the online pursuit. This may be the reason that use of AOL IM is a statistically significant and positive predictor of cyberstalking victimization.

Past research examining the victimization of college students has generally reported that exposure increases victimization across a variety of types of victimization (Fisher et al., 1998, 2002; Mustaine & Tewksbury, 1999, 2002). The current study adds to this body of work, reaffirming the importance of exposure in increasing college students' risks of victimization, and adds a new type of victimization to the list – cyberstalking.

Online Guardianship

Lifestyle-routine activities theory postulates that all else equal, more guarded or protected targets are less likely to be victimized, and that the presence of guardians reduces criminal opportunities and discourages offenders from taking advantage of opportunities. In the current study, online guardianship was measured by asking respondents if they use online profile trackers designed to monitor who is viewing their information, and by asking if they have their online social network accounts set to limited or private access. Neither of these measures of online guardianship produced results in accord with theoretical expectations. First, use of a profile tracker is *positively* associated with cyberstalking victimization rather than being associated with less exposure and harm. As previously discussed, it is possible that this effect is a methodological artifact of the survey question. In the survey, the question measuring whether the respondent used an online profile tracker did not specify whether this form of online guardianship was adopted as a result of previous problems encountered online (e.g., unwanted messages, harassment), or whether a profile tracker was being used before, during, or after a victimization incident. As a result, it is difficult to determine whether use of such an online device increases or decreases risks for cyberstalking. Second, having one's online profile set to limited access did not significantly affect risks of victimization for any of the cyberstalking variables. Considering these two findings, the current study does not find support for the LRAT concept of guardianship in reducing victimization. This finding is not entirely surprising as previous studies examining college student victimization in both physical space and cyberspace have produced mixed results on the effects of guardianship (Bossler & Holt, 2009; Fisher et al., 1998; Marcum, 2009; Mustaine & Tewksbury, 1999). Reynald (2009) and Tillyer and Eck (2009) have also pointed out that the guardianship component of routine activities theory is in need of further attention from researchers, and the current study findings support this conclusion regarding the need for greater sophistication in the measurement of guardianship and its consequences for victimization.

Online Proximity
Adding strangers as friends to one's online social networks was positively correlated with every type of pursuit except threats of violence, and it is rather clear why this would be the case. As an example, if a potential stalker is online browsing profiles on Facebook or Myspace (or some other online social network) and comes across a profile picture of someone he/she finds attractive, they can send a request to that person to be added as one of their online friends. If the target agrees to this request, that potential stalker can now view, access, or download any of the material the victim has posted on their online profile. This aspect of the social network platform enables the potential cyberstalker to see what that person is writing about (e.g., what they are going to do that day), potentially what their contact information is (if the victim has that information listed online), what their interests are, their relationship status, as well as other information that would be useful in pursuing and becoming more attached to the victim. The strong and consistent effect of online proximity across types of victimization may also explain the lack of statistically significant findings for the target attractiveness and guardianship variables. While a possible victim may have information posted about themselves online (i.e., target attractiveness), the stalker cannot view or make use of this information unless the victim has granted them access. Not granting unwanted parties as friends can also be considered a form of self-guardianship.

According to the proximity element of lifestyle-routine activities theory, increased physical proximity to motivated offenders results in an increase in crime and victimization. As was argued in Chapter 4, the idea of proximity can be transitioned from physical space to online networks, and the results of the current study suggest online proximity to motivated offenders does increase likelihood of cyberstalking victimization. These results are in accord with previous work examining the victimization of college students from a LRAT perspective (Fisher et al., 1998; Mustaine & Tewksbury, 1998, 1999, 2002).

Target Attractiveness
Target attractiveness, as it was conceived in the current study, did not affect the likelihood of cyberstalking victimization. As mentioned previously, this could well be the result of the difficulty in operationalizing the theoretical concept (Dunham & Monk, 2009). Indeed, in past work involving college student victimization, only Fisher and colleagues (1998, 2002) have reported effects of target attractiveness in accord with theoretical predictions. It may be that the current measures of target attractiveness simply do not gauge what makes one an attractive target for cyberstalkers adequately. It may also be that, as argued above, online proximity and allowing strangers access to personal information simply matters a great deal more in predicting victimization than does target attractiveness. The positive and statistically significant bivariate relationship (r_{pb} = .154, $p \leq$ .01) between these two variables indicates that more attractive targets may also be more likely to grant strangers access to their online information. More work is clearly needed in exploring this theoretical concept, especially as it pertains to online types of victimization (Dunham & Monk, 2009). To date, the current study represents the first attempt at examining the effects of target attractiveness in predicting cyberstalking or cybervictimization.

Online Deviance
As previously discussed, engaging in risky activities (i.e., deviant lifestyles) has emerged as a key risk factor for a variety of types of victimization (e.g., Jensen & Brownfield, 1987; Lauritsen et al., 1991; Sampson & Lauritsen, 1990), and it appears that cyberstalking victimization is no exception. Consistent with previous work examining the cybervictimization of college students (Choi, 2008; Bossler & Holt, 2009; Holt & Bossler, 2009), online deviance (i.e., persistently contacting others, harassing others, making unwanted sexual advances toward

others, threatening others, hacking, illegally downloading materials online, and engaging in the sending/receiving of sexually provocative images via text message) is a strong predictor of five of the six victimization variables (the exception being identity fraud[32]). Participating in these sorts of activities not only represents a deviant lifestyle, but it exposes these individuals to others who are participating in the same kinds of activities; that proximity allows for the possibility of these individuals being victimized themselves (i.e., opportunity). These results not only add further support to the hypothesis that participation in deviant or risky lifestyles and routine activities increases the likelihood of victimization, but also highlight the fact that such activities among college students increase the likelihood of cyberstalking victimization.

Low Self-Control
Finally, an underlying propensity toward low self-control was expected to affect cyberstalking victimization in two ways: (1) individuals who have low self-control are hypothesized to take fewer precautions when engaging in online activities (e.g., they may be more likely to visit risky websites or allow strangers access to their personal information); and (2) those with low self-control might be more likely to be aggressive, argumentative, or rude in their online interactions with others, making them targets of online victimization through harassment or issuance of threats. Those with low self-control are also hypothesized to be more likely to engage in deviant and risky activities online, as indicated by the statistically significant bivariate relationship between online deviance and low self-control ($r = 0.115$, $p \leq 0.001$). However, the low self-control variable operated as expected only for one dependent variable – unwanted contact. That low self-control did not affect likelihood of victimization for the other types of cyberstalking victimization or identity fraud victimization as expected may be the result of how the concept was operationalized. In the future, more accepted and convention measures of low self-control should be used in studying cyberstalking

---

[32]This suggests that there are different opportunity structures for cyberstalking as compared to identity fraud.

victimization to determine whether low self-control affects the likelihood of cybervictimization.

Summary of Risk Factors for Cyberstalking
In summary, the key questions to be addressed are: who is victimized online and why? Based on the results presented in Chapter 5, there are certain demographic groups whose members are disproportionately victimized, and there are certain lifestyles and routine activities that put individuals at risk for cyberstalking victimization. Consistent with theory, those who are exposed to motivated offenders, those who come into online proximity with motivated offenders, and those who engage in online deviance themselves are most at risk for becoming cybercrime victims. In addition, females and those with deviant peers are more likely to experience cyberstalking. Attention now turns to an assessment of how well lifestyle-routine activities theory can explain the victimization of college students in cyberspace environments.

Lifestyle-Routine Activities Theory and Cyberstalking
The lifestyle-routine activities perspective is the preeminent theory in victimology, but has thus far not been extensively applied to cybervictimization. Thus, one of the key questions this study sought to answer was whether the theory could be applied fruitfully to online types of victimization, and specifically cyberstalking. In Chapter 4 it was argued that each of the core concepts in the theory (i.e., exposure, proximity, guardianship, target attractiveness, deviant lifestyles, and low self-control) could be adapted to virtual environments. However, while each of the concepts found an online counterpart, not all of them proved to be significantly related to victimization. Interestingly, guardianship and target attractiveness (as they were operationalized here) did not influence the likelihood of cybervictimization as expected[33]. Therefore, the results suggest only moderate support for the utility of lifestyle-routine activities theory in explaining cyberstalking; however, it is clear that more work is needed to come to a more complete assessment of this theory in application to cybercrimes. The following section discusses how some of the arguments against applying the theory to cybercrimes can be reconciled.

---

[33] In this case, online guardianship was positively related to victimization.

Cyberlifestyle-Routine Activities Theory

Yar (2005) has argued that routine activities theory cannot make a theoretical transition to cyberspace. While acknowledging that some of the core concepts such as motivated offenders and guardianship find an online counterpart, he argues that other aspects of applying the theory to cybercrimes cannot be reconciled (Yar, 2005: 424). His main argument against a cyberlifestyle-routine activities theory is that routine activities theory is premised on the intersection in *time* and *space* of victims and offenders in facilitating environments, and in cyberspace this convergence is less apparent. Yar has written in this regard:

> "...whereas people, objects and activities can be clearly located within relatively fixed and ordered spatio-temporal configurations in the "real world", such orderings appear to destabilize in the virtual world. In other words, the routine activity theory holds that the "organization of time and space is central" for criminological explanation (Felson 1998: 148), yet the cyber-spatial environment is chronically spatio-temporally *disorganized*. The inability to transpose RAT's postulation of 'convergence in space and time' into cyberspace thereby renders problematic its straightforward explanatory application to the genesis of cybercrimes" (Yar, 2005: 424).

Yar's point is very well-taken. Clearly, as it is conventionally articulated, the theory does not make a straightforward transition to explain crimes in cyberspace. Nonetheless, in my view the core theoretical concepts and the notion that the three essential elements of a crime (i.e., victims, offenders, environments) intersect to create criminal opportunities can indeed be adapted to crimes involving cyberspace networks.

As was argued in Chapter 3, cybercrimes need to be thought of as network problems, meaning that victims and offenders do not come together in physical space but instead interact through cyberspace networks (Eck & Clarke, 2003). Networks can facilitate this "coming together" of victims and offenders for a variety of types of crime, ranging from telemarketing scams, to mail fraud, to a range of cybercrimes. This reconceptualizing of the place element in routine activities theory as a cyberspace network however, does not end the discussion. To say that a cyberspace network alone is a proxy for a place is analogous to saying that a victim and offender being in the same state or the same country is enough to satisfy the criteria of the victim and offender intersecting in space. Clearly, victims and offenders can be part of the same cyberspace network and never manifest opportunities for victimization. For this reason, it is useful to consider places in terms of specific virtual domains, such as websites.

For instance, conceptually it makes good sense to think of a specific chat room or an online social networking site such as Myspace as a specific place for cyberstalking to occur. This can be done rather than considering "the Internet" as a place with respect to the place of crime occurrence. Further, online places are more manageable with respect to limiting opportunities for victimization through manipulation of the virtual environment (Reyns, 2010). This is the case because it is a simpler proposition to design crime prevention measures into a virtual domain through web design, security, and programming than it is to redesign physical environments with landscape modifications and brick and mortar.

The theoretical transition of the place element from physical space, to networks, to online places seems quite reasonable; however, these changes do not address Yar's second criticism—namely, that of the temporal divergence of victims and offenders. As an example, say a cyberstalker sends a threatening message to his victim through a social networking page. The victim may not be online to receive the message. Indeed, the victim may not know that they've been sent a message for hours, days, or even weeks, eliminating the traditional conception of an intersection between victim and offender in real time. However, in this scenario the threatening message is still waiting for the victim, and when the recipient does eventually check their messages the victim and offender's action will intersect in time. The victim and offender may not interact in the "traditional" sense (i.e., face-to-face); instead, the offender acts and waits for the victim to experience the intent of the act (i.e., the outcome or cyberstalking incident will have transpired).

Figure 6.1 depicts this asynchronous intersection of victims and offenders in online environments. Note that the conditions under which the victim and offender converge are entirely contingent on both the place/network as well as an overlap in time. This overlap in time where there is this action and reaction may be very near (e.g., AOL IM, Skype) or the time lag may be considerable. The shaded inner triangle indicates the opportunity for a cybercrime such as cyberstalking to occur. Figure 6.1 may also prove a useful tool for applying lifestyle-routine activities to other types of crime in which the victim and offender do not physically meet (e.g., various types of frauds, such as Nigerian money schemes).

Figure 6.1: The Asynchronous Intersection of Victims and Offenders in Online Environments

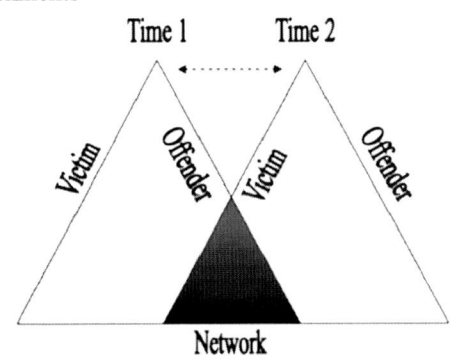

In sum, based on the results of the current study (e.g., the effects of online exposure, online proximity, and online deviance on overall cyberstalking victimization), lifestyle-routine activities theory can be modified to explain online types of victimization. As Tillyer and Eck (2009) have argued:

> "Routine activities theory focuses on offenders making contact with targets at places. Some crimes, however, involve 'crime at a distance.' Mail bombers, for example, do not come close to their targets. Internet fraudsters are able to steal from victims from anywhere in the world. Either routine activities theory is limited to place-based crimes or it needs revision" (Tillyer & Eck, 2009: 286).

The authors further suggest that Eck and Clarke's (2003) substitution of *systems* for *places* solves the problem. The current study, therefore, supports Tillyer and Eck's (2009) call for revising routine activities theory to explain crime and victimization within systems rather than restricting the theory solely to crimes transpiring within traditional conceptions of place. As the authors point out, research on routine activities in systems is still in its very early stages, and consequently the current study makes an important contribution to this small body of research in testing the application of lifestyle-routine activities theory in cyberspace (a system). The next section addresses how cyberstalking victimization might be prevented in the future by reducing opportunities for victimization.

PREVENTING CYBERSTALKING BY REDUCING OPPORTUNITIES

Knowing what puts individuals at risk for victimization has obvious implications for preventing victimization in the future. One strategy for reducing cyberstalking victimization is to remove opportunities for it to occur (Reyns, 2010). The foremost method for doing so is situational crime prevention, which is a scientific method for reducing opportunities for crime (Clarke, 2010). By manipulating the immediate situation or environment in which crimes occur, and focusing on very specific forms of crime, this method has proven to be successful in reducing a number of types of crime (e.g., see Clarke, 1980, 1983, 1997). There are 25 commonly practiced techniques of situational crime prevention grouped into five broad categories, including: (1) increasing the effort involved to commit the crime; (2) increasing the risks associated with engaging in the crime; (3) reducing the rewards associated with carrying out the crime; (4) reducing provocations to commit the crime; and, (5) removing excuses for rationalizing the crime (Cornish & Clarke, 2003).

This study has identified several factors which increase the likelihood of cyberstalking victimization. Specifically, the number of open social networking accounts, the number of daily updates to these accounts, use of AOL Instant Messenger, use of an online profile tracker, allowing strangers to gain access to one's online information, engaging in online deviance, and possessing low self-control were all positive predictors of cyberstalking victimization. Table 6.1 presents some preventive tactics – grounded in situational crime prevention, prior research on cyberstalking, and the results of the current study – for reducing opportunities for cyberstalking victimization. In terms of increasing the effort involved in committing the crime, individuals can control who has access to their personal information online, they can limit their online exposure, and they can limit their online proximity to motivated offenders. Increasing the risk can be accomplished by reporting unwanted contacts to online place managers, such as website administrators or service providers. Rewards can be reduced by minimizing the exposure of one's personal information online, by keeping personal information vague, and by deflecting unwanted attempts at communication (e.g., block the user's attempts at communication through filters). Reducing provocations can be accomplished by not reciprocating when contacted unless it is to inform the other party (the cyberstalker) to cease communications, and by ensuring that the cyberstalker is not intentionally provoked through name-calling or being sent an unintended message (e.g., that the victim may be romantically interested). Excuses can be removed by making it clear to the cyberstalker that the repeated contacts or pursuit behaviors are unwanted and unacceptable, and by avoiding risky environments.

Table 6.1: Using Situational Crime Prevention to Limit Opportunities for Cyberstalking

Increase the Effort	Increase the Risks	Reduce the Rewards	Reduce Provocations	Remove Excuses
Control access to online information	Report unwanted contact	Minimize exposure of personal information	Do not escalate interactions	Do not mislead the cyberstalker
Limit online exposure	Make it easier to report cyberstalking	Keep personal information vague	Do not reciprocate	Avoid risky cyber-environments
Limit online proximity	Improve surveillance of cyber-environments	Deflect unwanted communications	Control problem users	Provide a code of conduct

Third parties can also play a role in reducing opportunities for cyberstalking victimization. Those who have influence over the routine activities of places are called *place managers* (Eck, 1994), and these individuals could feature prominently in preventing cybercrimes such as cyberstalking. Sampson, Eck, and Dunham (2010) suggested that controllers[34] (i.e., guardians, handlers, and place managers) sometimes fail in their supervision/protection responsibilities, and when that happens crimes are more likely to be carried out successfully. The authors argue that other parties (such as people, organizations, or institutions) called *super controllers* ultimately provide the incentives for controllers, thereby regulating crime.

Figure 6.2: The New Crime Triangle

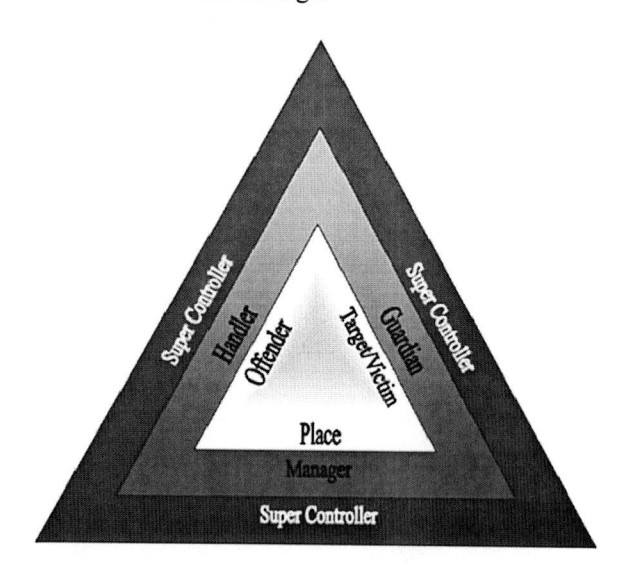

Source: Adapted from Sampson, Eck, and Dunham (2010).

Figure 6.2 illustrates the relationship between controllers and super controllers as suggested by Sampson, et al. (2010). According to the

---

[34] Controllers are those who discourage crime (e.g., security guards, bystanders) and have varying degrees of responsibility and effectiveness in doing so (Clarke, 1992; Felson, 1995).

authors, there are a number of types of super controllers depending upon the prospective crime scenario (e.g., organizations, media, different types of markets), but an example related to the prevention of cyberstalking may be those decision-makers that set the agenda for Internet providers and companies which maintain websites. A programmer or web designer may have some level of control over what transpires within the website for which they are responsible, making them a place manager for that website. However, they are restricted by the tools they are provided and the constraints placed upon them by their superiors; these superiors are "super controllers." Ultimately, online place managers and super controllers may have a large role to play in preventing cybercrimes. Table 6.1 provides ideas for online place managers and super controllers for preventing cyberstalking victimization. For example, it is possible to make it easier to report problem behaviors online, to improve surveillance in cyber-environments (e.g., monitoring sites for misuse), to control problem users (e.g., restricting access to site or services), and to provide a code of conduct for site users (i.e., to remove excuses).

LIMITATIONS

The results reported in this study should be considered in light of the limitations of the data collected. Certain methodological choices raise four issues that potentially limit the usefulness of the study's results: (1) the response rate; (2) temporal order considerations; (3) the measure of low self-control; and, (4) the possible overlap/cross-over between physical stalking and cyberstalking. Regarding the response rate, as was argued in Chapter 3, while it is not uncommon to receive a low response rate for a web-based survey (e.g., Couper, 2000; Dillman et al., 2009), this does not mean that the usual dangers associated with low response rates (e.g., lack of generalizability) are inconsequential. In addition, the sample was drawn from a single urban university in the Midwest, further limiting the generalizability to post-secondary student populations. Therefore, the results reported here should be approached with some caution along with an eye for their utility.

The second issue that potentially limits the results is temporal order of the relationships among the variables. Namely, while the measures of cyberstalking victimization are unbounded (i.e., lifetime prevalence of victimization), the measures of the independent variables (e.g., time online, number of parties attended) are temporally bounded (e.g., within the last month). This allows for the possibility that the relationships between variables with different time referents do not operate in the manner in which they appear. An example of this problem is the effect of guardianship on cyberstalking, a case in which the guardianship measure (using a profile tracker) actually increased likelihood of victimization. As previously discussed, it may be that adopting such guardianship measures was a reaction to a previous victimization as opposed to an antecedent to cyberstalking victimization.

The third noteworthy limitation is the measure of low self-control used here. As was described in Chapter 3, Grasmick et al.'s (1993) 24-item scale for measuring self-control was not utilized in the current study. Instead, fewer survey questions measuring some of the primary behaviors associated with low self-control were used, and reliability of the survey items used to construct the measure was somewhat low by traditional scale construction standards (Cronbach's $\alpha = 0.55$). There are two possible explanations for the weak predictive performance of low self-control in the current study: (1) either the survey items used to construct the measure do not adequately reflect the theoretical concept; or (2) the effects of low self-control manifest themselves differently in online environments.

A final issue that needs to be addressed as a limitation is the crossover between physical stalking and cyberstalking. The study was designed to measure those online behaviors that may act as risk factors for online victimization. However, it also makes sense that online victimization may be influenced by one's offline lifestyle. While these effects were controlled, measures of physical stalking were not collected. In the future, it would be beneficial to explore this possible crossover between physical lifestyles/routine activities, online lifestyles/routine activities, physical stalking, and cyberstalking.

FUTURE RESEARCH

The acknowledged limitations also provide opportunities for improvements in future research. The next step in studying cyberstalking should be to make methodological improvements in the areas discussed above, particularly in attaining higher response rates, using more conventional and tested measures of self-control, and developing bounded measures of victimization. Further, the sample used in the current study was drawn from a single urban university located in the Midwest. In the future it would be beneficial to expand to other universities and other populations to understand more fully the cyberstalking victimization of college students. Moreover, the data presented in the current study represent a single point in time, and ideally longitudinal data are desirable in establishing causal relationships. Therefore, succeeding studies in cyberstalking would benefit from obtaining longitudinal data.

Perhaps most critical to advancing the field of cyberstalking research is a need for work that examines the links between physically proximal stalking and cyberstalking. As was explained in Chapter 1, it is not clear whether cyberstalking is different that physically proximal stalking. It is true that mechanically it is different (electronic devices are used to pursue the victim), but many questions remain unanswered. Is cyberstalking an extension of behaviors that first transpire offline? Are there differences in lifestyle, self-control, or deviance among cybercrime victims? Among cyberstalkers? Future research should strive to answer these questions, as such answers would not only inform the cyberstalking knowledge base but add significantly to the stalking literature as well.

Future researchers may also consider expanding on or testing the revised lifestyle-routine activities theory as proposed in the current study. As argued by Tillyer and Eck (2009), the rethinking of some types of crimes as systems problems is an untapped source for future research on routine activities theory (Eck & Clarke, 2003). The current study has taken Eck and Clarke's (2003) model a step further by also addressing the issue of time with respect to the intersection in time and space of motivated offenders and suitable targets in facilitating environments. The lifestyle-routine activities model utilized in the current study has demonstrated some potential in explaining not only Internet-based crimes, but any crime committed at a distance (i.e., systems crimes).

CONCLUDING REMARKS

If the results presented in this study are representative of the cyberstalking victimization of college students in the United States generally, then it is clear that cyberstalking is a problem in need of attention, both administratively by universities and legally by policy makers. Although the measure of cyberstalking employed in the study was based on lifetime prevalence of victimization, for the majority of the sample their lifetime Internet use is likely only about ten years or so. The finding that over 40% of the sample experienced one or more types of online pursuit in this short amount of time suggests that, as with the growth of technologies that facilitate the crime, cyberstalking is likely to increase substantially, particularly among young people such as college students (Parsons-Pollard & Moriarty, 2009). Further, the state laws that prohibit behaviors such as cyberstalking not only differ from state to state, but tend to be overly broad. And, this lack of clarity creates difficulties for victims, law enforcement, and prosecutors alike as they struggle to respond to the problem. While not examined in the current study, cyberstalking also has harmful consequences, creating a number of psychological and emotional responses in the victims of this crime (Parsons-Pollard & Moriarty, 2009). According to Karjane, Fisher, & Cullen (2002), university policies governing stalking and cyberstalking behaviors are either inadequate or do not exist, and considering the prevalence of victimization suggested by this study and the daily growth of technologies and networks to facilitate the crime, this is an issue that may soon be difficult for universities to ignore. For all of these reasons, more work is needed in measuring, responding to, and understanding the consequences of cyberstalking. Only then can cybercrime laws and university policies address the issue based on empirical evidence.

Appendices

Appendix 1: States with Cyberstalking-Related Laws[35] and Inclusion of Fear in Definition of Cyberstalking

State	Mention of Fear	Requirement of Fear
Alabama	Yes	Yes
Alaska	No	No
Arizona	Yes*	No
Arkansas	Yes	No
California	Yes	Yes
Colorado	Yes*	No
Connecticut	Yes*	No
Delaware	Yes*	No
District of Columbia	Yes*	No
Florida	Yes*	Yes
Georgia	Yes	Yes
Hawaii	Yes*	No
Idaho	Yes	No
Illinois	Yes*	No
Indiana	Yes*	No
Iowa	Yes*	No
Kansas	Yes	Yes
Kentucky	Yes*	Yes
Louisiana	Yes*	No
Maine	Yes*	No
Maryland	No	No
Massachusetts	Yes	Yes

---

[35] The state either has a cyberstalking law or a harassment or stalking law covering cyberstalking.

Appendix 1 (Continued): States with Cyberstalking-Related Laws[36] **and Inclusion of Fear in Definition of Cyberstalking**

State	Mention of Fear	Requirement of Fear
Michigan	No	No
Minnesota	Yes	Yes
Mississippi	Yes*	No
Missouri	No	No
Montana	Yes*	No
Nebraska	Yes*	Yes
Nevada	No	No
New Hampshire	Yes*	No
New Jersey	Yes	No
New Mexico	Yes	Yes
New York	Yes*	No
North Carolina	Yes*	No
North Dakota	Yes	Yes
Ohio	No	No
Oklahoma	Yes	Yes
Oregon	Yes	Yes
Pennsylvania	Yes*	No
Rhode Island	Yes*	No
South Carolina	Yes*	Yes
South Dakota	Yes	No
Tennessee	No	No
Texas	Yes*	No
Utah	Yes*	Yes
Vermont	Yes	No
Virginia	Yes*	Yes
Washington	Yes*	No
West Virginia	Yes*	Yes
Wisconsin	No	No
Wyoming	Yes*	Yes
Total	43	18

*Indicates some variation of the word fear such as "a feeling of serious alarm" or "severe emotional distress."

Note on Appendix 1: If a state included a number of conditions for legally defining an incident as stalking (among them fear) that may not be akin to the emotional state of fear (such as annoyance), the *Re-*

---

[36] The state either has a cyberstalking law or a harassment or stalking law covering cyberstalking.

quirement of Fear column listed above was marked "no." For example, Texas' statute begins "A person commits an offense if, with intent to harass, annoy, alarm, abuse, torment, or embarrass another…" In this case, the Texas statute provides for a number of behaviors that will be considered stalking and does not necessarily require "fear," "alarm," or "torment" as a necessary condition of cyberstalking.

Source: WHOA (2009). Retrieved June 20, 2009,
http://www.haltabuse.org/resources/laws/index.shtml
National Center for Victims of Crime, Stalking Resource Center (2009). Retrieved June 27, 2009,
http://www.ncvc.org/src/main.aspx?dbID=DB_State-byState_Statutes117

Appendix 2: Cyberstalking Survey Consent Form

University of Cincinnati
Participant Information Sheet for a Research Study
College of Education, Criminal Justice, and Human Services:
Department of Criminal Justice
Billy Henson, M.S.
513-556-2617 (hensonb@email.uc.edu)
Brad Reyns, M.S.
513-556-2617 (reynsbw@email.uc.edu)

<u>**Online Social Networks: A New Arena for Victimization**</u>

We are inviting you to participate in a first-of-its-kind research study examining the phenomena of online social networks and blogs. As part of our doctoral dissertation research, this survey will ask questions about your use of the Internet and online social networks/blogs, as well as any annoyances and/or dangers you have encountered online. This survey is designed to allow undergraduate college students to speak out about any negative online experiences they have had, and it will serve as the basis for the examination of the possible threats of online social networks/blogs.

You were randomly selected to participate in this research study, along with 10,000 of your fellow students. Participation in this survey will take 10-20 minutes of your time. Your responses will be both password and firewall protected, and will be made available only to the researchers. Once you have finished the survey, your participation will be complete, and you will not be contacted further. In addition, your personal identification information, including your email address, will not be associated with your responses in an effort to preserve your anonymity. There is no payment or direct benefits to you for participation.

PARTICIPATION IN THIS RESEARCH STUDY IS STRICTLY VOLUNTARY, AND YOU HAVE THE OPTION OF QUITTING AT ANY TIME. Participation or non-participation will not affect any legal rights that you would normally have. If, in the event you feel upset or emotionally distressed as a result of the information you provided for this survey, you do have the option of contacting the University Counseling Center, 316 Dyer Hall (513-556-0648).

If you have any questions about the survey or study, you are welcome to contact us. The University of Cincinnati Institutional Review Board - Social and Behavioral Sciences reviews all non-medical research projects that involve human participants to be sure the rights and welfare of participants are protected. If you have questions about your rights as a research participant, you may contact the University of Cincinnati Institutional Review Board - Social and Behavioral Sciences at (513) 558-5784. If you have a concern about the study you may also call the UC Research Compliance Hotline at (800) 889-1547, or you may write to the Institutional Review Board-Social and Behavioral Sciences, G-28 Wherry Hall, ML 0567, 3225 Eden Avenue, PO Box 670567, Cincinnati, OH 45267-0567, or you may email the IRB office at irb@ucmail.uc.edu. The results of the survey are scheduled to be made available in June of 2010; please contact the investigators listed at the top of this page for more information.

By taking this survey, you are indicating your consent for your answers to be used for research study. Please print a copy of this Information Sheet for your records.

Appendix 3: 1st Wave Email Invitation

Subject Line: Online Social Networks Research Project

Hello Fellow UC Student,
As part of our doctoral dissertation research, we are inviting you to participate in a first-of-its-kind survey examining the phenomena of online social networks and blogs, such as Myspace and Facebook. You will be asked questions about your use of the Internet and online social networks/blogs, as well as any annoyances and/or dangers you have encountered online including any possible cyberstalking incidents. This survey is essential for our dissertation work, which is a requirement for graduation, and we greatly appreciate your help. If you have any questions, please let us know. Thank you so much for your participation!

To participate in our study, please follow the link below:

http://www.zoomerang.com/Survey/?p=WEB2292ZKV4NAY

Sincerely,
Billy Henson, M.S.
Department of Criminal Justice

Brad Reyns, M.S.
Department of Criminal Justice

Appendix 4: 2nd Wave Email Invitation

Subject Line: Online Social Networks Research Project
Hello Fellow UC Student,
As college students, we often help each other out. We are asking for a few minutes of your time to complete a survey that will help us carry out our doctoral dissertation research.

We invite you to participate in a first-of-its-kind survey examining the phenomena of online social networks and blogs, such as MySpace and Facebook. Questions ask about your use of the Internet and online social networks/blogs, as well as any annoyances and/or dangers you have encountered online including any possible cyberstalking incidents.

Your responses are essential for us to finish our degree. We greatly appreciate your help. If you have any questions, please let us know. If you have previously completed the survey, please disregard this email. Thank you so much for your participation!

To participate in our study, please follow the link below:

http://www.zoomerang.com/Survey/?p=WEB2295WEYVCCG

Sincerely,
Billy Henson, M.S.
Department of Criminal Justice

Brad Reyns, M.S.
Department of Criminal Justice

Appendix 5: Final Wave Email Invitation

Subject Line: Online Social Networks Research Last Call
Hello Fellow UC Student,
We have previously invited you to participate in our study of online social networks and related phenomena. This is our third and final wave of invitations. We are asking for more students to participate because we have fallen short of our target response goal. Your responses are essential for us to finish our degrees. We hope you will help us.

We are asking for a few minutes of your time to complete a survey that will help us carry out our doctoral dissertation research. The survey should take about 15 minutes. Questions ask about your use of the Internet and online social networks/blogs, as well as any annoyances and/or dangers you have encountered online including any possible cyberstalking incidents.

We greatly appreciate your help. If you have any questions, please let us know. If you have previously completed the survey, please disregard this email. Thank you so much for your participation!

To participate in our study, please follow the link below:

http://www.zoomerang.com/Survey/?p=WEB2295WEYVCCG

Sincerely,

Billy Henson, M.S.
Department of Criminal Justice

Brad Reyns, M.S.
Department of Criminal Justice

Appendix 6: Cyberstalking Survey Instrument

Questions marked with an asterisk (*) are necessary to complete the survey.

1. *Would you like to continue with the survey?
    - Yes
    - No

   (If yes, survey continues; if no, survey ends)

2. What is your gender?
    - Male
    - Female

3. *What is your age?
    - Under 18
    - 18
    - 19
    - 20
    - 21
    - 22
    - 23
    - 24
    - Over 24

   (If 18 – 24, survey continues; if no, survey ends)

4. What is your race/ethnicity?
    - American Indian
    - Asian/Pacific Islander
    - African American
    - Hispanic
    - White
    - Other/Unknown

5. What is your grade/class standing?
   - Freshman
   - Sophomore
   - Junior
   - Senior
   - Graduate
   - Other

6. What is your sexual orientation?
   - Heterosexual/Straight
   - Gay/Lesbian
   - Bisexual
   - Other

7. What is your current relationship status?
   - Single
   - Casual Dating
   - Long-Term Dating
   - Married/Living with Someone
   - Divorced/Separated/Widowed

8. Where do you live during the school year?
   - On-Campus Housing
   - Off-Campus University Housing
   - Off-Campus Non-University Housing
   - Home of Parent/Legal Guardian or Relative

9. With whom do you live during the school year? *(Check all that apply)*
   - Live Alone
   - Student Roommate(s)
   - Non-Student Roommate(s)
   - Romantic Partner/Significant Other
   - Parents
   - Other Relatives

10. What clubs/organizations do you participate in regularly?
    (*Check all that apply*)
    - University Athletic Teams
    - Greek Organizations
    - Honorary Organizations
    - Religious Organizations
    - Major/Department Organizations
    - None
    - Other, please specify

11. Did you transfer from another college/university?
    - Yes
    - No

12. Which of the following best describes your cumulative undergraduate grade point average?
    - Below 0.67
    - 0.67 - 1.66
    - 1.67 – 2.66
    - 2.67 – 3.66
    - 3.67 – 4.0

13. Since beginning school at UC, how many days/nights do you go to parties in an average month?
    - 0 – 30

14. Since beginning school at UC, how many days/nights do you go to bars or clubs in an average month?
    - 0 – 30

15. Since beginning school at UC, how many alcoholic drinks do you have in a average week?
    - 0 – 50

16. Since beginning school at UC, how many times do you use drugs in a average week?
   o   0 – 50

17. Please choose the characteristics that best describe you:

1	2
Yes	No
Outgoing	
Easy going	
Easily Upset	
Quiet	
Stubborn	
Friendly	
Intimidating	
Apologetic	
Sympathetic	
Perceptive	

18. Please indicate the most appropriate response to the statements below:

1	2	3	4
Strongly Agree	Agree	Disagree	Strongly Disagree
I consider myself to be cautious.			
I consider myself to be argumentative.			
I have trouble controlling my temper.			
I always devote time to studying.			
I often confront people when they make me upset.			
I consider myself to be a risk-taker.			
I spend a lot of time thinking about my future.			
I have a lot of money charged on credit cards.			

19. Please indicate the most appropriate response to the statements below:

1	2	3	4
Strongly Agree	Agree	Disagree	Strongly Disagree
I value my mother's opinion.			
I value my father's opinion.			
I like to spend time with my family.			
I frequently talk to my family.			
I value my friends' opionions.			
I like to spend time with my friends.			
I frequently talk to my friends.			

20. Do you use the Internet in your home/room?
    - Yes
    - No

21. Where else do you access the Internet? *(Please Check All That Apply)*
    - School Library
    - School Computer Lab
    - Work/Office
    - Parents/Relatives' Home
    - Classroom
    - School Food Court
    - Public Library
    - Coffee Shop/Café
    - PDA/Blackberry
    - Cell Phone
    - Other, please specify

22. On average, how much time do you actively spend online each day? (*Including Email, IM, Blogs, etc.*)
    - Less Than 1 Hour
    - 1 Hour
    - 2 Hours
    - 3 Hours
    - 4 Hours
    - 5 Hours
    - 6 Hours
    - 7 Hours
    - 8 Hours
    - 9 Hours
    - 10 Hours
    - 11 Hours
    - 12 Hours
    - 13 Hours
    - 14 Hours
    - 15 Hours
    - 16 Hours or More

23. What forms of electronic communication do you frequently use? (*Please Check All That Apply*)
    - Instant Messengers (AIM, Yahoo Messenger, etc.)
    - Email
    - Chat Rooms
    - Social Network/Blog Sites (Facebook, MySpace, Twitter etc.)
    - Text Messaging (Cell Phone, PDA, etc.)
    - Online Video Games
    - Other, please specify

24. What is the most frequent method you use to communicate with your family/friends?
    - In Person
    - Over the Phone
    - Online
    - Other

Appendices

25. What percentage of your friends would you estimate frequently use some type of online communication? (*Example: Instant Messenger, Social Networks, etc.*)
    o   0 – 100 (increments of 5)

26. What percentage of your friends would you estimate that you talk to online, in a average week? (*Example: Instant Messenger, Social Networks, etc.*)
    o   0 – 100 (increments of 5)

PLEASE INDICATE IF YOU HAVE USED ANY OF THE FOLLOWING FORMS OF ONLINE COMMUNICATION TO PERFORM THE DESCRIBED ACTIVITIES.

27. Have you ever flirted with a friend or aquaintance, WITH the intention or hope of pursuing a romantic or sexual relationship, including just hooking up?

	1	2
	Yes	No
Social Network/Blog		
Instant Messenger		
Email		
Other		

28. Have you ever flirted with a friend or acquaintance, WITHOUT the intention or hope of pursuing a romantic or sexual relationship, including just hooking up?

	1	2
	Yes	No
Social Network/Blog		
Instant Messenger		
Email		
Other		

29. Have you ever flirted with someone you didn't know, WITH the intention or hope of pursuing a romantic or sexual relationship, including just hooking up?

	1	2
	Yes	No
Social Network/Blog		
Instant Messenger		
Email		
Other		

30. Have you ever flirted with someone you didn't know, WITHOUT the intention or hope of pursuing a romantic or sexual relationship, including just hooking up?

	1	2
	Yes	No
Social Network/Blog		
Instant Messenger		
Email		
Other		

31. Have you ever hooked up (had brief sexual encounter) with someone you met online?

	1	2
	Yes	No
Social Network/Blog		
Instant Messenger		
Email		
Other		

Appendices

32. * Do you, or have you in the past, regularly use a social network/blog account? (*Example: MySpace, Facebook, Livejournal, etc.*)
    - o Yes
    - o No

    (If yes, survey continues with question 33; if no, skips to question 68)

SOCIAL NETWORK ACTIVITY SECTION

ALL OF THE FOLLOWING QUESTIONS ARE REGARDING ONLY SOCIAL NETWORK ACTIVITY. THE FOLLOWING QUESTIONS REFER TO ACTIVITY/COMMUNICATION THROUGH MYSPACE, FACEBOOK, LIVEJOURNAL, ETC.

33. How long have you had a social network/blog account?
    - o 1 Month or Less
    - o 3 – 117 Months (increments of 3)
    - o 120 Months or More (10 Years)

34. How many social network/blog accounts have you opened, even if you don't use them regularly?
    - o 1 – 14
    - o 15 or More

35. What type of social network/blog account do you have? (*Please Check All That Apply*)
    - o Bebo
    - o Classmates.com
    - o Facebook
    - o Friendster
    - o Livejournal
    - o MySpace
    - o Orkut
    - o Twitter

- Windows Live Spaces
- Xanga
- Other, please specify

36. Why did you open a social network/blog account? (*Please Check All That Apply*)
    - Curiosity
    - To Keep in Touch with Family/Friends
    - To Meet New Friends
    - To Meet New Romantic Partners
    - To Flirt
    - Live Out Fantasy Online
    - Other, please specify

37. How accurate (honest) is the information on your account?
    - Completely False
    - Mostly False with Some Truth
    - Mostly True with Some Exaggeration
    - Completely True

38. In an average week, how many times do you update the information on your social network/blog account(s)?
    - 0 – 24
    - 25 or More

39. How many friends would you estimate you have in total on all your online social network/blog account(s)?
    (open ended)

40. In an average day, how many hours do you spend on your social network/blog site(s)?
    - Less Than 1 Hour
    - 1 Hour
    - 2 Hours
    - 3 Hours
    - 4 Hours
    - 5 Hours
    - 6 Hours
    - 7 Hours
    - 8 Hours

- o 9 Hours
- o 10 Hours
- o 11 Hours
- o 12 Hours
- o 13 Hours
- o 14 Hours
- o 15 Hours
- o 16 Hours or More

41. What percentage of your friends would you estimate also have social network/blog accounts?
    - o 0 – 100 (increments of 5)

42. Which of the following do you include on your social network/blog account(s)? (*Please Check All That Apply*)
    - o First Name
    - o Full Name
    - o Nickname
    - o Birth Date
    - o Relationship Status
    - o Sexual Orientation
    - o Home Town
    - o School Address
    - o Home Address
    - o Job Title
    - o Work Name
    - o Work Address
    - o Instant Messenger ID
    - o Email Address
    - o Home Phone Number
    - o Cell Phone Number
    - o School Name
    - o Academic Major
    - o Class Schedule
    - o Clubs/Organizations

- Address for Other Social Network/Blog Sites
- Interests/Activities
- Photos
- Videos
- Top Friends
- Networks
- Notes/Blogs
- Applications
- Other, please specify

43. Have you ever posted a profile picture of yourself on your social network/blog account?
    - Yes
    - No

44. Have you ever posted photos on your social network/blog account, other than a profile picture?
    - Yes
    - No

45. How many photos would you estimate that you have on your social network/blog account?
    (open ended)

46. What types of places are the people in your posted photos typically at? (*Please Check All That Apply*)
    - Room/Apartment/Home
    - Work
    - Restaurants
    - Sporting Events
    - Extra-Curricular Activities
    - Parties
    - Bars and Clubs
    - Outdoor Activities (*Ex: Camping, Swimming, etc.*)
    - Other, please specify

47. Have you ever posted any of the following type of photos on your social network/blog account, even if you were only joking around in the pictures?

	1	2
	Yes	No
You and/or Your Friends Drinking Alcohol		
You and/or Your Friends Doing Drugs		
You and/or Your Friends Doing Things That You Would Consider Sexually Provocative (*Ex: Nudity, Sexual Poses, etc.*)		

48. Have you ever described any of the following interests or experiences on your social network/blog account?

	1	2
	Yes	No
Experiences with Alcohol Use		
Experiences with Drug Use		
Sexual Experiences, Interests, or Fantasies		

49. Have you ever joined a club/group through your social network/blog account that encourages any of the following activities?

	1	2
	Yes	No
Drinking Alcohol		
Using Drugs		
Having Sex		

50. Have you ever added someone as friend whom you didn't know?
    o Yes
    o No

51. Have you ever communicated with someone through other forms of electronic communication that you first met on your social network/blog account? (Example: *IM, Email, Text Messenging, etc.*)
    o Yes
    o No

52. Have you ever met someone in person that you met for the first time on your social network/blog account?
    o Yes
    o No

53. Have you ever dated someone in person that you met for the first time on your social network/blog account?
    o Yes
    o No

54. Do you have your social network/blog account set to private or limited access?
    o Yes
    o No

55. Have you ever joined an online service that assists you in acquiring new friends for your social network/blog account? (Example: *Friendtrain, Whoretrain, Pimptrain, etc.*)
    o Yes
    o No

56. Have you ever used an online program that allows you to update multiple social network accounts at once? (Example: *ping.fm*)
    o Yes
    o No

57. Have you ever used or tried to use a profile tracker that keeps track of who views your account? (Example: *Trakzor*)
    o Yes
    o No

58. How likely do you think it is that someone you had/have an intimate relationship with will use the information on your social network/blog to do any of the following?

1	2	3	4	5	6	7	8	9	10
Not Likely at All									Very Likely
Harass You									
Stalk You									
Threaten to Physically Harm You									

59. How likely do you think it is a friend or acquaintance will use the information on your social network/blog to do any of the following?

1	2	3	4	5	6	7	8	9	10
Not Likely at All									Very Likely
Harass You									
Stalk You									
Threaten to Physically Harm You									

60. How likely do you think it is that a stranger will use the information on your social network/blog to do any of the following?

1	2	3	4	5	6	7	8	9	10
Not Likely at All									Very Likely
Harass You									
Stalk You									
Threaten to Physically Harm You									

61. How afraid are you that someone you had/have an intimate relationship with will use the information on your social network/blog to do any of the following?

1	2	3	4	5	6	7	8	9	10
Not Likely at All									Very Likely
Harass You									
Stalk You									
Threaten to Physically Harm You									

62. How afraid are you that a friend or acquaintance will use the information on your social network/blog to do any of the following?

1	2	3	4	5	6	7	8	9	10
Not Likely at All									Very Likely
Harass You									
Stalk You									
Threaten to Physically Harm You									

63. How afraid are you that a stranger will use the information on your social network/blog to do any of the following?

1	2	3	4	5	6	7	8	9	10
Not Likely at All									Very Likely
Harass You									
Stalk You									
Threaten to Physically Harm You									

64. Has anyone ever hacked into your social network/blog account?
    o Yes
    o No
    o Unsure

Appendices

65. Has anyone ever hacked into one of your friend's social network/blog account?
    - o Yes
    - o No
    - o Unsure

66. Has anyone ever opened a social network/blog account posing as you?
    - o Yes
    - o No
    - o Unsure

67. Has anyone ever opened a social network/blog account posing as one of your friends?
    - o Yes
    - o No
    - o Unsure

Questions marked with an asterisk (*) are necessary to complete the survey.

ONLINE ACTIVITY SECTION

ALL OF THE FOLLOWING QUESTIONS ARE REGARDING ONLINE ACTIVITY, OTHER THAN SOCIAL NETWORK/BLOG ACCOUNT(S) ACTIVITY, SUCH AS ACTIVITY/COMMUNICATION WITH INSTANT MESSENGERS, EMAIL, TEXT MESSENGING, ETC.

68. Do you regularly use any of the following online sites/groups? (Please Check All That Apply)
    - o YouTube
    - o Yahoo Groups
    - o Google Groups
    - o Match.com

- eHarmony
- AOL Instant Messenger (AIM)
- Other, please specify

69. * Have you ever posted photos/videos online?
    - Yes
    - No

    (If yes, continues to question 70; if no, skips to question 73)

70. If so, who do you typically post photos/videos of online? (Please Check All That Apply)
    - Yourself
    - Your Family
    - Your Boyfriend/Girlfriend
    - Your Ex-Boyfriend/Girlfriend
    - Your Spouse/Partner
    - Your Ex-Spouse/Partner
    - Friends of the Same Sex as You
    - Friends of the Opposite Sex as You
    - Other, please specify

71. What types of places are the people in your posted photos/videos typically at? (Please Check All That Apply)
    - Room/Apartment/Home
    - Work
    - Restaurants
    - Sporting Events
    - Extra-Curricular Activities (Example: Organization Meetings)
    - Parties
    - Bars and Clubs
    - Outdoor Activities (Example: Camping)
    - Other, please specify

72. Have you ever posted any of the following type of photos/video online, even if you were only joking around? (Please check all that apply)
    - You and/or Your Friends Drinking Alcohol
    - You and/or Your Friends Doing Drugs

Appendices

- o You and/or Your Friends Acting Sexually Provocative (Example: Kissing, Nudity, etc.)
- o None of the Above

73. Have you ever met someone in person that you first met on online?
    - o Yes
    - o No

74. Have you ever dated someone that you first met on online?
    - o Yes
    - o No

75. Have you ever described interests or experiences with any of the following online?

	1	2
	Yes	No
Alcohol Use		
Drug Use		
Sexual Experiences, Interests, or Fantasies		

76. Has anyone ever hacked into any of your online programs? (*Ex: Email, Instant Messenger, etc.*)
    - o Yes
    - o No
    - o Unsure

77. Has anyone ever hacked into any of your friends' online programs? (*Ex: Email, Instant Messenger, etc.*)
    - o Yes
    - o No
    - o Unsure

78. Has anyone ever pretended to be you online, without your permission?
    - Yes
    - No
    - Unsure

79. Has anyone ever pretended to be one of your friends online, without their permission?
    - Yes
    - No
    - Unsure

80. How likely do you think it is that someone you had/have an intimate relationship with will use an online program (Ex. *Instant Messenger, Email, etc.*) to do any of the following?

1	2	3	4	5	6	7	8	9	10
Not Likely at All									Very Likely
Harass You									
Stalk You									
Threaten to Physically Harm You									

81. How likely do you think it is a friend or acquaintance will use an online program (Ex. *Instant Messenger, Email, etc.*) to do any of the following?

1	2	3	4	5	6	7	8	9	10
Not Likely at All									Very Likely
Harass You									
Stalk You									
Threaten to Physically Harm You									

82. How likely do you think it is that a stranger will use an online program (Ex. *Instant Messenger, Email, etc.*) to do any of the following?

1	2	3	4	5	6	7	8	9	10
Not Likely at All									Very Likely
Harass You									
Stalk You									
Threaten to Physically Harm You									

83. How afraid are you that someone you had/have an intimate relationship with will use an online program (Ex. *Instant Messenger, Email, etc.*) to do any of the following?

1	2	3	4	5	6	7	8	9	10
Not Likely at All									Very Likely
Harass You									
Stalk You									
Threaten to Physically Harm You									

84. How afraid are you that a friend or acquaintance will use an online program (Ex. *Instant Messenger, Email, etc.*) to do any of the following?

1	2	3	4	5	6	7	8	9	10
Not Likely at All									Very Likely
Harass You									
Stalk You									
Threaten to Physically Harm You									

85. How afraid are you that a stranger will use an online program (Ex. *Instant Messenger, Email, etc.)* to do any of the following?

1	2	3	4	5	6	7	8	9	10
Not Likely at All									Very Likely
Harass You									
Stalk You									
Threaten to Physically Harm You									

Questions marked with an asterisk (*) are necessary to complete the survey.

86. * Has anyone ever contacted you or attempted to contact you <u>on more than one occasion</u> online after you asked/told them to stop?
    - Yes
    - No

    (If yes, opens incident report; if no, continues to question 87)

Incident Report

1. * How many different people have contacted you or attempted to contact you on more than one occasion online after you asked/told them to stop?
    - 1 – 4
    - 5 or more

    (An incident report is filled out for each incident up to five)

2. How did you know the person that contacted or attempted to contact you? (*Ex: Husband, Ex-Wife, Girlfriend, Ex-Boyfriend, Friend, Former Friend, Stranger, etc.*) <u>Please Do Not Put Names</u>
    (open ended)

3. How long have you known that person?
    - N/A
    - Less Than 1 Month
    - 1 – 120 Months
    - More Than 120 Months

4. How many times did that person contact or attempt to contact you after you asked/told them to stop?
    - o 1 – 99
    - o 100 or More

5. How long did that person contact or attempt to contact you after you asked/told them to stop? (*Ex: 2 weeks, 4 months, etc.*) (open ended)

6. How did that person contact or attempt to contact you? (*Please Check All That Apply*)
    - o Social Network/Blog Message Board/Wall
    - o Social Network/Blog Messenger Program
    - o Email
    - o Instant Messenger
    - o Text Message
    - o Telephone
    - o Letter
    - o In Person
    - o Other, please specify

7. Did that person's actions cause you to fear for your personal safety?
    - o Yes
    - o No

8. How afraid were you?

1	2	3	4	5	6	7	8	9	10
Not Afraid									Very Afraid

9. What did you do as a result of that person repeatedly contacting or attempting to contact you? (*Check All That Apply*)
    - Ignore Him/Her
    - Tell Your Friends or Relatives
    - Report the Incident to the Social Network/Blog Provider
    - Report the Incident to University Staff
    - Report the Incident to the Police
    - Confront that Person Online
    - Confront that Person Face-to-Face/Over the Phone
    - Set Account to Private or Limited
    - Block that Person
    - Nothing
    - Other, please specify

Questions marked with an asterisk (*) are necessary to complete the survey.

87. * Has anyone ever persistently harassed or annoyed you on more than one occasion online?
    - Yes
    - No

(If yes, opens incident report; if no, continues to question 88)

Incident Report

1. * How many different people have persistently harassed or annoyed you on more than one occasion online?
    - 1 – 4
    - 5 or more

(An incident report is filled out for each incident up to five)

2. How did you know the person that persistently harassed or annoyed you? (*Ex: Husband, Ex-Wife, Girlfriend, Ex-Boyfriend, Friend, Former Friend, Stranger, etc.*) Please Do Not Put Names
(open ended)

Appendices

3. How long have you known that person?
   - N/A
   - Less Than 1 Month
   - 1 – 120 Months
   - More Than 120 Months

4. How many times did that person persistently harass or annoy you?
   - 1 – 99
   - 100 or More

5. How long did that person persistently harass or annoy you? (*Ex: 2 weeks, 4 months, etc.*) (open ended)

6. Through what means did that person persistently harass or annoy you? (*Please Check All That Apply*)
   - Social Network/Blog Message Board/Wall
   - Social Network/Blog Messenger Program
   - Email
   - Instant Messenger
   - Text Message
   - Telephone
   - Letter
   - In Person
   - Other, please specify

7. Did that person's actions cause you to fear for your personal safety?
   - Yes
   - No

8. How afraid were you?

1	2	3	4	5	6	7	8	9	10
Not Afraid									Very Afraid

9. What did you do as a result of that person persistently harassing or annoying you?
    - Ignore Him/Her
    - Tell Your Friends or Relatives
    - Report the Incident to the Social Network/Blog Provider
    - Report the Incident to University Staff
    - Report the Incident to the Police
    - Confront that Person Online
    - Confront that Person Face-to-Face/Over the Phone
    - Set Account to Private or Limited
    - Block that Person
    - Nothing
    - Other, please specify

Questions marked with an asterisk (*) are necessary to complete the survey.

88. * Has anyone ever made unwanted sexual advances toward you <u>on more than one occasion</u> online?
    - Yes
    - No

    (If yes, opens incident report; if no, continues to question 89)

Incident Report

1. * How many different people have made unwanted sexual advances toward you on more than one occasion online?
    - 1 – 4
    - 5 or more

    (An incident report is filled out for each incident up to five)

2. How did you know the person that made unwanted sexual advances toward you? (*Ex: Husband, Ex-Wife, Girlfriend, Ex-Boyfriend, Friend, Former Friend, Stranger, etc.*) <u>Please Do Not Put Names</u>
(open ended)

Appendices

3. How long have you known that person?
   - N/A
   - Less Than 1 Month
   - 1 – 120 Months
   - More Than 120 Months

4. How many times did that person make unwanted sexual advances toward you?
   - 1 – 99
   - 100 or More

5. How long did that person make unwanted sexual advances toward you? (*Ex: 2 weeks, 4 months, etc.*) (open ended)

6. Through what means did that person make unwanted sexual advances toward you? (*Please Check All That Apply*)
   - Social Network/Blog Message Board/Wall
   - Social Network/Blog Messenger Program
   - Email
   - Instant Messenger
   - Text Message
   - Telephone
   - Letter
   - In Person
   - Other, please specify

7. Did that person's actions cause you to fear for your personal safety?
   - Yes
   - No

8. How afraid were you?

1	2	3	4	5	6	7	8	9	10
Not Afraid									Very Afraid

9. What did you do as a result of that person making unwanted sexual advances toward you?
    - Ignore Him/Her
    - Tell Your Friends or Relatives
    - Report the Incident to the Social Network/Blog Provider
    - Report the Incident to University Staff
    - Report the Incident to the Police
    - Confront that Person Online
    - Confront that Person Face-to-Face/Over the Phone
    - Set Account to Private or Limited
    - Block that Person
    - Nothing
    - Other, please specify

Questions marked with an asterisk (*) are necessary to complete the survey.

* Has anyone ever spoken to you in a violent manner or threatened to physically harm you <u>on more than one occasion</u> online?
    - Yes
    - No

(If yes, opens incident report; if no, continues to question 90)

Incident Report

1. * How many different people have spoken to you in a violent manner or threatened to physically harm you on more than one occasion online?
    - 1 – 4
    - 5 or more

(An incident report is filled out for each incident up to five)

2. How did you know the person that spoke to you in a violent manner or threatened to physically harm you? (*Ex: Husband, Ex-Wife, Girlfriend, Ex-Boyfriend, Friend, Former Friend, Stranger, etc.*) <u>Please Do Not Put Names</u>
(open ended)

Appendices

3. How long have you known that person?
   - N/A
   - Less Than 1 Month
   - 1 – 120 Months
   - More Than 120 Months

4. How many times did that person speak to you in a violent manner or threaten to physically harm you?
   - 1 – 99
   - 100 or More

5. How long did that person continue to speak to you in a violent manner or threaten to physically harm you? (*Ex: 2 weeks, 4 months, etc.*) (open ended)

6. Through what means did that person speak to you in a violent manner or threaten to physically harm you? (*Please Check All That Apply*)
   - Social Network/Blog Message Board/Wall
   - Social Network/Blog Messenger Program
   - Email
   - Instant Messenger
   - Text Message
   - Telephone
   - Letter
   - In Person
   - Other, please specify

7. Did that person's actions cause you to fear for your personal safety?
   - Yes
   - No

8. How afraid were you?

1	2	3	4	5	6	7	8	9	10
Not Afraid									Very Afraid

9. What did you do as a result of that person speaking to you in a violent manner or threatening to physically harm you?
    - Ignore Him/Her
    - Tell Your Friends or Relatives
    - Report the Incident to the Social Network/Blog Provider
    - Report the Incident to University Staff
    - Report the Incident to the Police
    - Confront that Person Online
    - Confront that Person Face-to-Face/Over the Phone
    - Set Account to Private or Limited
    - Block that Person
    - Nothing
    - Other, please specify

89. Please indicate if you have participated in any of the following activities:

	1	2
	Yes	No
Repeatedly contacted or attempted to contact someone online after they asked/told you to stop.		
Repeatedly harassed or annoyed someone online after they asked/told you to stop.		
Repeatedly made sexual advances toward someone online after they asked/told you to stop.		
Repeatedly spoken to someone in a violent manner or threatened to physically harm them online after they asked/told you to stop.		
Attempted to hack into someone's online social network account.		
Downloaded music or movies illegally.		
Sent sexually explicit images to someone online or through text messaging.		
Received sexually explicit images from someone online or through text messaging.		

THANK YOU FOR YOUR PARTICIPATION!

If you have any questions about the survey or study, you are welcome to contact us. The results of the survey are scheduled to be made available in June of 2011; please contact the investigators listed below for more information.

Department of Criminal Justice

Billy Henson, M.S. 513-556-2617 (hensonb@email.uc.edu)
Brad Reyns, M.S. 513-556-2617 (reynsbw@email.uc.edu)

If you have any questions about your rights as a research participant, you may call the Chair of the Institutional Review Board—Social and Behavioral Sciences at 558-5784.

FOR MORE INFORMATION OR ADDITIONAL RESOURCES:

If you feel emotionally distressed as a result of this survey or if you would like more information about the University Counseling Center, please follow this link: University Counseling Center

If you would like more information on the prevalance of and/or the services available for stalking victimization, please visit The National Center for Victims of Crime or The Stalking Victims' Sanctuary.

Appendix 7: Survey Items Used to Construct the Dependent and Independent Variables, Survey Items, Coding, and Cronbach's α

VICTIMIZATION VARIABLES

Contact
Has anyone ever contacted you or attempted to contact you <u>on more than one occasion</u> online after you asked/told them to stop?

Responses recoded as: 0 = Nonvictim, 1 = Victim

Harassment
Has anyone ever persistently harassed or annoyed you <u>on more than one occasion</u> online?

Responses recoded as: 0 = Nonvictim, 1 = Victim

Unwanted Sexual Advances

Has anyone ever made unwanted sexual advances toward you <u>on more than one occasion</u> online?

Responses recoded as: 0 = Nonvictim, 1 = Victim

Threats of Violence

Has anyone ever spoken to you in a violent manner or threatened to physically harm you <u>on more than one occasion</u> online?

Responses recoded as: 0 = Nonvictim, 1 = Victim

Identity Fraud

Has anyone ever pretended to be you online, without your permission?

Responses recoded as: 0 = Nonvictim, 1 = Victim

Cyberstalking
Dichotomous measure of 0 = Nonvictim, 1 = Victim for any of the four types of online pursuit

INDEPENDENT VARIABLES

Online Exposure Variables

Time Online

On average, how much time do you actively spend online each day? (Including email, IM, blogs, etc.)

Responses recoded as: 0 to 16 hours or more

Number of Social Networks (SN)

How many social network/blog accounts have you opened, even if you don't use them regularly?

Responses coded as: 1 to 15 or more

Number of SN Updates

In an average week, how many times do you update the information on your social network/blogaccount(s)?

Responses coded as: 1 to 25 or more

Time on Social Network

In an average day, how many hours do you spend on your social network/blog site(s)?

Responses recoded as: 0 to 16 hours or more

Number of Photos on SN

How many photos would you estimate that you have on your social network/blog account?

Use AOL Instant Messenger

Do you regularly use any of the following online sites/groups? (Please check all that apply)
   Youtube
   Yahoo Groups
   Google Groups
   Match.com
   eHarmony
   AOL Instant Messenger (AIM)
   Other, please specify
   AIM variable recoded as: 0 = No, 1 = Yes

Online Guardianship Variables

SN Set to Private

Do you have your social network/blog account set to private or limited access?

Responses recoded as: 0 = No, 1 = Yes

Use a Profile Tracker

Have you ever used or tried to use a profile tracker that keeps track of who views your account?

Responses recoded as: 0 = No, 1 = Yes

Online Proximity Variables

Added Stranger as Friend

Have you ever added someone as a friend whom you didn't know?

Responses recoded as: 0 = No, 1 = Yes

Appendices

Number of Friends on SN

How many friends would you estimate you have in total on all your online social network/blog account(s)?

Friend Service

Have you ever used an online program that allows you to update multiple social network accounts at once?

Responses recoded as: 0 = No, 1 = Yes

Online Target Attractiveness

Which of the following do you include on your social network/blog account(s)?
  Full Name
  Relationship Status
  Sexual Orientation
  Instant Messenger ID
  Email Address
  Other Social Network Addresses
  Interests/Activities
  Photos
  Videos

Responses recoded as: 0 = No, 1 = Yes
Summed scale 0 – 9

Online Deviance

Please indicate if you have participated in any of the following activities:

Repeatedly contacted or attempted to contact someone online after they asked/told you to stop.
Repeatedly harassed or annoyed someone online after they asked/told you to stop.

Repeatedly made sexual advances toward someone online after they asked/told you to stop.

Repeatedly spoken to someone in a violent manner or threatened to physically harm them online after they asked/told you to stop.

Attempted to hack into someone's online social network account.

Downloaded music or movies illegally.

Sent sexually explicit images to someone online or through text messaging.

Received sexually explicit images from someone online or through text messaging.

Responses recoded as: 0 = No, 1 = Yes
Summed scale 0 – 8

Low Self-Control

Please indicate the most appropriate response to the statements below:
 I consider myself to be argumentative.
 I have trouble controlling my temper.
 I often confront people when they make me upset.
 I consider myself to be a risk-taker.

Responses recoded as: 1 = Strongly Disagree to 4 = Strongly Agree
Cronbach's $\alpha = 0.54$

CONTROL VARIABLES

Gender

What is your gender?

Responses recoded as: 0 = Male, 1 = Female

Age

What is your age?

Responses recoded as: 18 – 24

Race

What is your race/ethnicity?

Responses recoded as: 0 = White, 1 = Nonwhite

Non-single

What is your relationship status?

Responses recoded as: 0 = Single, 1 = Not Single

Deviant Peers

How likely do you think it is a friend or acquaintance will use an online program (e.g., Instant Messenger, Email, etc.) to do any of the following?
    Harass You
    Stalk You
    Threaten to Physically Harm You

Responses coded as: 1 = Not Likely at All to 10 = Very Likely
Cronbach's $\alpha = 0.80$

Risky Offline Lifestyle

Since beginning school at UC, how many days/nights do you go to parties in an average month?
    Responses coded as: 0 – 30

Since beginning school at UC, how many days/nights to you go to bars or clubs in an average month?
    Responses coded as: 0 – 50

Since beginning school at UC, how many alcoholic drinks do you have in an average week?

Responses coded as: 0 – 50
Cronbach's $\alpha = 0.67$

Appendix 8: Collinearity Diagnostics

Variable	Tolerance	VIF
Gender	0.803	1.246
Age	0.933	1.071
Nonwhite	0.898	1.114
Non-single	0.916	1.092
Peer Deviance	0.923	1.083
Risky Offline Activities	0.825	1.213
Time Online	0.702	1.424
Number of Social Networks	0.784	1.275
Number SN Updates	0.805	1.242
Time on Social Network	0.608	1.645
Number of Photos on SN	0.789	1.268
AOL IM	0.854	1.171
SN Set to Private	0.936	1.068
Use a Profile Tracker	0.854	1.171
Added Stranger as Friend	0.911	1.097
Number of Friends on SN	0.804	1.244
Friend Service	0.942	1.062
Target Attractiveness	0.800	1.251
Online Deviance	0.866	1.155
Low Self-Control	0.921	1.086

References

Alexy, E.M., Burgess, A.W., Baker, T., & Smoyak, S.A. (2005). Perceptions of cyberstalking among college students. *Brief Treatment and Crisis Intervention, 5,* 2 79-289.

Allison, P.D. (2001). *Missing Data.* Thousand Oaks, CA: Sage.

Amir, M. (1971). *Patterns in Forcible Rape.* Chicago: University of Chicago Press.

Ashcroft, J. (2001). *Stalking and Domestic Violence: Report to Congress.* Washington, D.C.: US Department of Justice, Office of Justice Programs.

Baum, K., Catalano, S., Rand, M., & Rose, K. (2009). *Stalking Victimization in the United States.* Washington, D.C.: US Department of Justice.

Bjerregaard, B. (2000). An empirical study of stalking victimization. *Violence and Victims, 15,* 389-405.

Bocij, P. (2003). Victims of cyberstalking: An exploratory study of harassment perpetrated via the Internet. *First Monday, 8.* Retrieved June 26, 2009, from http://firstmonday.org/htbin/cgiwrap/bin/ojs/index.php/fm/article/view/1086/1006.

Bocij, P. (2006). *Cyberstalking: Harassment in the Internet Age and How to Protect your Family.* Westport, CT: Praeger Publishers.

Bocij, P., & McFarlane, L. (2002a). Cyberstalking: Genuine problem or public hysteria? *Prison Service Journal, 140,* 32-39.

Bocij, P., & McFarlane, L. (2002b). Online harassment: Towards a definition of cyberstalking. *Prison Service Journal, 139,* 31-38.

Bocij, P., & McFarlane, L. (2003a). Cyberstalking: A matter for community safety – but the numbers do not add up. *Community Safety Journal, 2,* 26-34.

Bocij, P., & McFarlane, L. (2003b). Seven fallacies about cyberstalking. *Prison Service Journal, 149,* 37-42.

Bossler, A.M., & Holt, T.J. (2009). On-line activities, guardianship, and malware infection: An examination of routine activities theory. *International Journal of Cyber Criminology, 3,* 400-420.

Bossler, A.M., & Holt, T.J. (2010). The effect of self-control on victimization in the cyberworld. *Journal of Criminal Justice, 38,* 227-236.

Bossler, A.M., Holt, T.J., & May, D.C. (2011). Predicting online harassment victimization among a juvenile population. *Youth & Society.* DOI: 10.1177/0044118X11407525

Brantingham, P., & Brantingham, P. (1995). Crime generators and crime attractors. *European Journal on Criminal Policy & Research, 3,* 5-26.

Buhi, E.R., Clayton, H., & Surrency, H.H. (2009). Stalking victimization among college women and subsequent help-seeking behaviors. *Journal of American College Health, 57,* 419-425.

Cass, A.I. (2007). Routine activities and sexual assault: An analysis of individual- and school-level factors. *Violence and Victims, 22,* 350-366.

Choi, K. (2008). Computer crime victimization and integrated theory: An empirical assessment. *International Journal of Cyber Criminology, 2,* 308-333.

Clarke, R.V. (1980). Situational crime prevention: Theory and Practice. *British Journal of Criminology, 20,* 136-147.

Clarke, R.V. (1983). Situational crime prevention: Its theoretical basis and practical scope. In M. Tonry, & N. Morris (Eds.), *Crime & Justice: An Annual Review of Research,* Vol. 4, (pp. 225-256). Chicago: University of Chicago Press.

Clarke, R.V., (Ed.). (1997). *Situational Crime Prevention: Successful Case Studies.* Guilderland, NY: Harrow and Heston.

Clarke, R.V. (1997). Introduction. In R.V. Clarke (Ed.), *Situational Crime Prevention: Successful Case Studies.* Guilderland, NY: Harrow and Heston.

Clarke, R.V. (1999). *Hot products: Understanding, Anticipating and Reducing Demand for Stolen Goods.* London: Home Office.

Clarke, R.V. (2004). Technology, criminology and crime science. *European Journal on Criminal Policy and Research, 10,* 55-63.

Clarke, R.V. (2010). Situational crime prevention. In B.S. Fisher & S.P. Lab, (Eds.), *Encyclopedia of Victimology and Crime Prevention* (pp. 879-883). Thousand Oaks, CA: Sage.

Cohen, L.E., & Felson, M. (1979). Social change and crime rate trends: A routine activity approach. *American Sociological Review, 44,* 588-608.

Cohen, L.E., Felson, M., & Land, K.C. (1980). Property crime rates in the United States: A macrodynamic analysis, 1947-1977 with ex ante forecasts for the mid-1980s. *American Journal of Sociology, 86,* 90-118.

Cohen, L.E., Kluegel, J.R., & Land, K.C. (1981). Social inequality and predatory criminal victimization: An exposition and test of a formal theory. *American Sociological Review, 46,* 505-524.

Cook, P.J. (1986). The demand and supply of criminal opportunities. In M. Tonry, & N. Morris (Eds.), *Crime and Justice: A Review of Research*, vol. 7 (pp. 1-27). Chicago: University of Chicago Press.

Cornish, D., & Clarke, R.V. (2003). Opportunities, precipitators and criminal decisions: A reply to Wortley's critique of situational crime prevention. In M.J. Smith, & D. Cornish (Eds.), *Theory for Practice in Situational Crime Prevention*, Vol. 16, (pp. 41-96). Monsey, NY: Criminal Justice Press.

Couper, M.P. (2000). Web surveys: A review of issues and approaches. *Public Opinion Quarterly, 64,* 464-494.

Cupach, W. R., & Spitzberg, B. H. (2004). *The Dark Side of Relationship Pursuit: From Attraction to Obsession and Stalking.* Mahwah, NJ: Erlbaum.

Davis, K.E., & Frieze, I.H. (2002). Research on stalking: What do we know and where do we go? In K.E. Davis, I.H. Frieze, & R.D. Maiuro (Eds.), *Stalking: Perspectives on Victims and Perpetrators* (pp. 353-375). New York: Springer Publishing Company, Inc.

Dillman, D.A. (2007). *Mail and Internet Surveys: The Tailored Design Method.* Hoboken, NJ: Wiley.

Dillman, D.A., Phelps, G., Tortora, R., Swift, K., Kohrell, J., Berck, J., & Messer, B.L. (2009). Response rate and measurement differences in mixed-mode surveys using mail, telephone, interactive voice response (IVR) and the Internet. *Social Science Research, 38,* 1-18.

Dillman, D.A., Smyth, J.D., & Christian, L.M. (2008). *Internet, Mail, and Mixed-mode Surveys: The Tailored Design Method.* Hoboken, NJ: Wiley.

Doerner, W.G. (2010). Victimology. In B.S. Fisher, & S.P. Lab (Eds.), *Encyclopedia of Victimology and Crime Prevention* (pp. 996-1,003). Thousand Oaks, CA: Sage.

D'Ovidio, R., & Doyle, J. (2003). A study on cyberstalking: Understanding investigative hurdles. *FBI Law Enforcement Bulletin, 73,* 10-17.

Dunham, J.R., & Monk, K.M. (2009, March). *Evolution or De-Evolution? Assessing Target Attractiveness: A Review of the Development and Measurement.* Poster session presented at the annual meeting of the Academy of Criminal Justice Sciences, Boston, MA.

Eck, J.E. (1994). Drug Markets and Drug Places: A Case-Control Study of the Spatial Structure of Illicit Drug Dealing. Doctoral dissertation, University of Maryland, College Park.

Eck, J.E. (2003). Police problems: The complexity of problem theory, research and evaluation. *Crime Prevention Studies,* vol. 15 (pp. 79-113). Monsey, NY: Criminal Justice Press.

Eck, J.E., & Clarke, R.V. (2003). Classifying common police problems: A routine activity approach. *Crime Prevention Studies,* vol. 16 (pp. 7-39). Monsey, NY: Criminal Justice Press.

Eck, J.E., Clarke, R.V., & Guerette, R.T. (2007). Risky facilities: Crime concentration in homogeneous sets of establishments and facilities. In G. Farrell, K.J. Bowers, S.D. Johnson, & M. Townsley (Eds.), *Crime Prevention Studies,* vol. 21 (pp. 225-264). Monsey, NY: Criminal Justice Press.

Ellison, L. (1999). Cyberstalking: Tackling harassment on the Internet. 14th BILETA Conference: "CYBERSPACE 1999: Crime, Criminal Justice and the Internet." Retrieved June 29, 2009, http://www.bileta.ac.uk/Document%20Library/1/Cyberstalking%20-%20Tackling%20Harassment%20on%20the%20Internet.pdf

Ellison, L, & Akdeniz, Y. (1998). Cyber-stalking: The regulation of harassment on the Internet. *Criminal Law Review, December Spe-*

cial Edition: Crime, Criminal Justice and the Internet, 29-48. Retrieved September 25, 2009, http://www.cyber-rights.org/documents/ talking_article.pdf

Englebrecht, C.M., & Reyns, B.W. (2011). Gender differences in acknowledgment of stalking victimization: Results from the NCVS stalking supplement. *Violence and Victims, 26,* 560-579.

Felson, M. (1995). Those who discourage crime. In J.E. Eck, & D. Weisburd (Eds.), *Crime and Place.* Crime prevention studies, vol. 4 (pp. 53-66). Monsey, NY: Criminal Justice Press.

Felson, M. (1998). *Crime and Everyday Life* (2nd Edition). Thousand Oaks, CA: Sage.

Felson, M. (2002). *Crime and Everyday Life* (3rd Edition). Thousand Oaks, CA: Sage.

Felson, M. (2008). Routine activity approach. In R. Wortley, & L. Mazerolle, (Eds.), *Environmental Criminology and Crime Analysis* (pp. 70-76). Portland, OR: Willan Publishing.

Felson, M., & Clarke, R.V. (1998). *Opportunity Makes the Thief: Practical Theory for Crime Prevention.* London: Home Office.

Field, A. (2005). *Discovering Statistics Using SPSS* (2nd Edition). Thousand Oaks, CA: Sage.

Finkelhor, D., & Asdigian, N. L. (1996). Risk factors for youth victimization: Beyond a lifestyle-routine activities approach. *Violence and Victims, 11,* 3-19.

Finkelhor, D., Mitchell, K.J., & Wolak, J. (2000). *Online Victimization: A Report on the Nation's Youth.* Washington, D.C.: US Department of Justice.

Finn, J. (2004). A survey of online harassment at a university campus. *Journal of Interpersonal Violence, 19,* 468-483.

Fisher, B.S. (2001). Being pursued and pursuing during the college years: Their extent, nature, and impact of stalking on college campuses. In J.A. Davis (Ed.), *Stalking Crimes and Victim Protection: Protection, Intervention, Threat Assessment, and Case Management* (pp. 207-238). Boca Raton: CRC Press LLC.

Fisher, B.S., Cullen, F.T., & Turner, M.G. (2000). *The Sexual Victimization of College Women.* Washington D.C.: US Department of Justice.

Fisher, B.S., Cullen, F.T., & Turner, M.G. (2002). Being pursued: Stalking victimization in a national study of college women. *Criminology & Public Policy, 1,* 257-308.

Fisher, B.S., Daigle, L.E., & Cullen, F.T. (2010a). *Unsafe in the Ivory Tower: The Sexual Victimization of College Women.* Thousand Oaks, CA: Sage.

Fisher, B.S., Daigle, L.E., & Cullen, F.T. (2010b). What distinguishes single from recurrent sexual victims? The role of lifestyle-routine activities and first-incident characteristics. *Justice Quarterly, 27,* 102-129.

Fisher, B.S., & Reyns, B.W. (2009). Victimization. In J.M. Miller (Ed.). *21st Century Criminology: A Reference Handbook* (pp. 162-172). Thousand Oaks, CA: Sage.

Fisher, B.S., Sloan, J.J., Cullen, F.T., Lu, C. (1998). Crime in the ivory tower: Level and sources of student victimization. *Criminology, 36,* 671-710.

Fisher, B.S., & Stewart, M. (2007). Vulnerabilities and opportunities 101: The extent, nature, and impact of stalking among college students and implications for campus policy and programs. In B.S. Fisher, J. Sloan III (Eds.), *Campus Crime: Legal, Social and Policy Issues,* (2nd edition) (pp. 210-230). Springfield, IL: Charles C. Thomas Publisher.

Fox, J.A., Levin, J., & Forde, D.R. (2009). *Elementary Statistics in Criminal Justice Research* (3rd Edition). Allyn & Bacon.

Fox, K.A., Gover, A.R., & Kaukinen, C. (2009). The effects of low self-control and childhood maltreatment on stalking victimization among men and women. *American Journal of Criminal Justice, 34,* 181-197.

Fox, K.A., Nobles, M.R., & Fisher, B.S. (2011). Method behind the madness: An examination of stalking measurements. *Aggression and Violent Behavior, 16,* 74-84.

Garofalo, J. (1987). Reassessing the lifestyle model of criminal victimization. In M.R. Gottfredson, & T. Hirschi (Eds.), *Positive Criminology* (pp. 23-42). Newbury Park, CA: Sage.

Garson, G.D. (2006). *Data Imputation for Missing Values.* Retrieved January 9, 2010,
http://faculty.chass.ncsu.edu/garson/PA765/missing.htm

Gottfredson, M.R. (1984). *Victims of Crime: The Dimensions of Risk.* London: Home Office.

Gottfredson, M.R., & Hirschi, T. (1990). *A General Theory of Crime.* Stanford, CA: Stanford University Press.

Grabosky, P.N. (2001). Virtual criminology: Old wine in new bottles? *Social and Legal Studies, 10,* 243-249.

Grabosky, P.N. (2007). *Electronic Crime.* Upper Saddle River, NJ: Pearson.

Grasmick, H.G., Tittle, C.R., Bursik, R.J., & Arneklev, B.J. (1993). Testing the core empirical implications of Gottfredson and Hirschi's general theory of crime. *Journal of Research in Crime and Delinquency, 30,* 5-29.

Henson, B. (2010). Cyberstalking. In B.S. Fisher & S.P. Lab, (Eds.), *Encyclopedia of Victimology and Crime Prevention* (pp. 253-256). Thousand Oaks, CA: Sage.

Henson, B. (2011). Fear of Crime Online: Examining the Effects of Online Victimization and Perceived Risk on Fear of Cyberstalking Victimization. Doctoral dissertation, University of Cincinnati.

Henson, B., Reyns, B.W., & Fisher, B.S. (2011). Security in the 21st century: Examining the link between online social network activity, privacy, and interpersonal victimization. *Criminal Justice Review, 36,* 253-268.

Henson, B., Wilcox, P., Reyns, B.W., & Cullen, F.T. (2010). Gender, adolescent lifestyles, and violent victimization: Implications for routine activity theory. *Victims & Offenders, 5,* 303-328.

Higgins, G.E. (2005). Can low self-control help with the understanding of the software piracy problem? *Deviant Behavior, 26,* 1-24.

Higgins, G.E., Ricketts, M.L., & Vegh, D.T. (2008). The role of self-control in college student's perceived risk and fear of online victimization. *American Journal of Criminal Justice, 33,* 223-233.

Hilinski, C.M. (2009). Fear of crime among college students: A test of the shadow of sexual assault hypothesis. *American Journal of Criminal Justice, 34,* 84-102.

Hindelang, M.J., Gottfredson M.R., & Garofalo, J. (1978). *Victims of Personal Crime: An Empirical Foundation for a Theory of Per-*

sonal Victimization. Cambridge, MA: Ballinger Publishing Company.

Holt, T.J., & Bossler, A.M. (2009). Examining the applicability of lifestyle-routine activities theory for cybercrime victimization. *Deviant Behavior, 30,* 1-25.

Holtfreter, K, Reisig, M.D., & Pratt, T.C. (2008). Low self-control, routine activities, and fraud victimization. *Criminology, 46,* 189-220.

Jaishankar, K., & Sankary, V.U. (2005). Cyber stalking: A global menace in the information super highway. *ERCES Online Quarterly Review, 2.* Retrieved June 28, 2009, http://www.erces.com/journal/Journal.htm

Jensen, G.F., & Brownfield, D. (1986). Gender, lifestyles, and victimization: Beyond routine activity. *Violence and Victims, 1,* 85-99.

Jerin, R., & Dolinsky, B. (2001). You've got mail! You don't want it: Cyber-victimization and on-line dating. *Journal of Criminal Justice and Popular Culture, 9,* 15-21.

Jordan, C.E., Wilcox, P., & Pritchard, A.J. (2007). Stalking acknowledgement and reporting among college women experiencing intrusive behaviors: Implications for the emergence of a "classic stalking case." *Journal of Criminal Justice, 35,* 556-569.

Karjane, H.M., Fisher, B.S., & Cullen, F.T. (2002). *Campus Sexual Assault: How America's Institutions of Higher Education Respond.* Final Report, NIJ Grant # 1999-WA-VX-0008. Newton, MA: Education Development Center, Inc.

Koch, L.Z. (n.d.). Cyberstalking hype. *Interactive Week.* Retrieved June 25, 2009, http://attrition.org/errata/media.html

Koops, B.J., & Leenes, R. (2006). Identity theft, identity fraud and/or identity-related crime: Definitions matter. *Datenschutz und Datensicherheit, 30,* 553-556.

Kraft, E.M., & Wang, J. (2010). An exploratory study of the cyberbullying and cyberstalking experiences and factors related to victimization of students at a public liberal arts college. *International Journal of Technoethics, 1,* 74-91.

Lasley, J.R. (1989). Drinking routines/lifestyles and predatory victimization: A causal analysis. *Justice Quarterly, 6,* 529-542.

Lauritsen, J.L., & Laub, J.H. (2007). Understanding the link between victimization and offending: New reflections on an old idea. In M. Hough, & M. Maxfield (Eds.), *Surveying Crime in the 21st Centu-*

ry, Crime prevention studies, vol. 22 (pp. 55-75). Monsey, NY: Criminal Justice Press.

Lauritsen, J. L., Laub, J. H., & Sampson, R. J. (1992). Conventional and delinquent activities: Implications for the prevention of violent victimization among adolescents. *Violence and Victims, 7,* 91-108.

Lauritsen, J. L., Sampson, R. J., & Laub, J. H. (1991). The link between offending and victimization among adolescents. *Criminology, 29,* 265-292.

Levrant Miceli, S., Santana, S.A., & Fisher, B.S. (2001). Cyberaggression: Safety and security issues for women worldwide. *Security Journal, 14,* 11-27.

Little, R.J.A., & Rubin, D.B. (2002). *Statistical Analysis with Missing Data,* (2nd Edition). Hoboken, NJ: John Wiley & Sons, Inc.

Lynch, J.P. (1987). Routine activity and victimization at work. *Journal of Quantitative Criminology, 3,* 283-300.

Marcum, C.D. (2009). *Adolescent Online Victimization: A Test of Routine Activities Theory.* El Paso, TX: LFB Scholarly Publishing.

Marcum, C.D., Higgins, G.E., & Ricketts, M.L. (2010a). Potential factors of online victimization of youth: An examination of adolescent online behaviors utilizing routine activity theory. *Deviant Behavior, 31,* 381-410.

Marcum, C.D., Ricketts, M.L., & Higgins, G.E. (2010b). Assessing sex experiences of online victimization: An examination of adolescent online behaviors using routine activity theory. *Criminal Justice Review, 35,* 412-437.

Massey, J.L., Krohn, M.D., & Bonati, L.M. (1989). Property crime and the routine activities of individuals. *Journal of Research in Crime and Delinquency, 26,* 378-400.

Maxfield, M.G. (1987). Lifestyle and routine activity theories of crime: Empirical studies of victimization, delinquency, and offender decision-making. *Journal of Quantitative Criminology, 3,* 275-282.

Maxwell, A. (2001). *Cyberstalking.* Master's thesis, Auckland University, Auckland, New Zealand. Retrieved June 26, 2009, http://www.netsafe.org.nz/ Doc_Library/cyberstalking.pdf.

McQuade, S.C. (2006). *Understanding and Managing Cybercrime.* Boston, MA: Allyn & Bacon.

Menard, S. (2002). *Applied Logistic Regression Analysis* (2nd Edition). Thousand Oaks, CA: Sage.

Menard, S. (2010). *Logistic regression: From introductory to advanced concepts and applications.* Thousand Oaks, CA: Sage.

Mendelsohn, B. (1976). Victimology and contemporary society's trends. *Victimology, 1,* 8-28.

Mertler, C.A., & Vannatta, R.A. (2005). *Advanced and Multivariate Statistical Methods: Practical Application and Interpretation* (3rd Edition). Glendale, CA: Pyrczak Publishing.

Messner, S.F. & Blau, J.R. (1987). Routine leisure activities and rates of crime: A macro-level analysis. *Social Forces, 65,* 1035-1052.

Miethe, T. D., & McDowall, D. (1993). Contextual effects in models of criminal victimization. *Social Forces, 71,* 741-759.

Miethe, T.D., & Meier, R.F. (1990). Opportunity, choice, and criminal victimization: A test of a theoretical model. *Journal of Research in Crime and Delinquency, 27,* 243-266.

Miethe, T.D., & Meier, R.F. (1994). *Crime and its Social Context: Toward an Integrated Theory of Offenders, Victims, and Situations.* Albany, NY: SUNY Press.

Miethe, T.D., Stafford, M.C., & Long, J.S. (1987). Social differentiation in criminal victimization: A test of routine activities/lifestyle theories. *American Sociological Review, 52,* 184-194.

Miethe, T.D., Stafford, M.C., & Sloane, D. (1990). Lifestyle changes and risks of criminal victimization. *Journal of Quantitative Criminology, 6,* 357-376.

Mustaine, E. E., & Tewksbury, R. (1998). Predicting risks of larceny theft victimization: A routine activity analysis using refined lifestyles measures. *Criminology, 36,* 829-858.

Mustaine, E.E., & Tewksbury, R. (1999). A routine activity theory explanation for women's stalking victimizations. *Violence Against Women, 5,* 43-62.

Mustaine, E. E., & Tewksbury, R. (2002). Sexual assault of college women: A feminist interpretation of a routine activities analysis. *Criminal Justice Review, 27,* 89-123.

Newman, O. (1996). *Creating Defensible Space.* U.S. Department of Housing and Urban Development.

Newman, G., & Clarke, R.V. (2003). *Superhighway Robbery: Preventing E-commerce Crime.* Portland, OR: Willan Publishing.

Nobles, M.R., Fox, K.A., Piquero, N., & Piquero, A.R. (2009). Career dimensions of stalking victimization and perpetration. *Justice Quarterly, 26,* 476-503.

Osgood, D.W., Wilson, J.K., O'Malley, P.M., Bachman, J.G., & Johnston, L.D. (1996). Routine activities and individual deviant behaviors. *American Sociological Review, 61,* 635-655.

Pampel, F.C. (2000). *Logistic Regression: A Primer.* Thousand Oaks, CA: Sage.

Parsons-Pollard, N., & Moriarty, L.J. (2008). Cyberstalking: What's the big deal? In L.J. Moriarty (Ed.), *Controversies in Victimology,* (2nd Edition) (pp. 103-113). Cincinnati: Anderson.

Parsons-Pollard, N., & Moriarty, L.J. (2009). Cyberstalking: Utilizing what we do know. *Victims and Offenders, 4,* 435-441.

Pathé, M.T., Mullen, P.E., & Purcell, R. (2000). Same-gender stalking. *Journal of the American Academy of Psychiatry and the Law, 4,* 191-197.

Piquero, A.R., MacDonald, J., Dobrin, A., Daigle, L.E., & Cullen, F.T. (2005). Self-control, violent offending, and homicide victimization: Assessing the general theory of crime. *Journal of Quantitative Criminology, 21,* 55-71.

Pittaro, M.L. (2008). Cyber stalking: An analysis of online harassment and intimidation. *International Journal of Cyber Criminology, 1,* 180-197.

Pratt, T.C., & Cullen, F.T. (2000). The empirical status of Gottfredson and Hirschi's General Theory of Crime: A meta-analysis. *Criminology, 38,* 931-964.

Pratt, T.C., Holtfreter, K., & Reisig, M.D. (2010). Routine online activity and Internet fraud targeting: Extending the generality of routine activity theory. *Journal of Research in Crime and Delinquency, 47,* 267-296.

Rand, M.R. (2008). *Criminal Victimization, 2008.* Washington, D.C.: US Department of Justice.

Reno, J. (1999). *Cyberstalking: A New Challenge for Law Enforcement and Industry.* U.S. Department of Justice. Retrieved June 25, 2009, http://www.usdoj.gov/criminal/cybercrime/cyberstalking.htm

Reynald, D.M. (2009). Guardianship in action: Developing a new tool for measurement. *Crime Prevention & Community Safety, 11*, 1-20.

Reyns, B.W. (2010). A situational crime prevention approach to cyberstalking victimization: Preventive tactics for Internet users and online place managers. *Crime Prevention & Community Safety, 12*, 99-118.

Reyns, B.W. (2011). Online routines and identity theft victimization: Further expanding routine activity theory beyond direct-contact offenses. *Journal of Research in Crime and Delinquency.* DOI: 10.1177/0022427811425539

Reyns, B.W., Burek, M.W., Henson, B., & Fisher, B.S. (2011). The unintended consequences of digital technology: Exploring the relationship between sexting and cybervictimization. *Journal of Crime and Justice.* DOI: 10.1080/0735648X.2011.641816

Reyns, B.W., & Englebrecht, C.M. (2010). The stalking victim's decision to contact the police: A test of Gottfredson and Gottfredson's theory of criminal justice decision making. *Journal of Criminal Justice, 38*, 998-1,005.

Reyns, B.W., Henson, B., & Fisher, B.S. (2011). Being pursued online: Applying cyberlifestyle-routine activities theory to cyberstalking victimization. *Criminal Justice and Behavior, 38*, 1,149-1,169.

Reyns, B.W, Henson, B., & Fisher, B.S. (2012). Stalking in the twilight zone: Extent of cyberstalking victimization and offending among college students. *Deviant Behavior, 33*, 1-25.

Sampson, R.J. (1987). Personal violence by strangers: An extension and test of the opportunity model of predatory victimization. *The Journal of Criminal Law & Criminology, 78*, 327-356.

Sampson, R., Eck, J.E., & Dunham, J. (2010). Super controllers and crime prevention: A routine activity explanation of crime prevention success and failure. *Security Journal, 23*, 37-51.

Sampson, R.J., & Lauritsen, J.L. (1990). Deviant lifestyles, proximity to crime, and the offender-victim link in personal violence. *Journal of Research in Crime and Delinquency, 27*, 110-139.

Sampson, R.J., & Wooldredge, J. (1987). Linking the micro- and macro- level dimensions of lifestyle-routine activities and opportunity models of predatory victimization. *Journal of Quantitative Criminology, 3*, 371-393.

Schafer, S. (1968). *The Victim and his Criminal: A Study in Functional Responsibility.* New York: Random House.

Schreck, C.J. (1999). Criminal victimization and low self-control: An extension and test of a general theory of crime. *Justice Quarterly, 16,* 633-654.

Schreck, C.J., & Fisher, B.S. (2004). Specifying the influence of family and peers on violent victimization: Extending routine activities and lifestyles theories. *Journal of Interpersonal Violence, 19,* 1021-1041.

Schreck, C.J., Stewart, E.A., & Fisher, B.S. (2006). Self-control, victimization, and their influence on risky lifestyles: A longitudinal analysis using panel data. *Journal of Quantitative Criminology, 22,* 319-340.

Schreck, C.J., Stewart, E.A., & Osgood, D.W. (2008). A reappraisal of the overlap of violent offenders and victims. *Criminology, 46,* 871-906.

Schreck, C.J., Wright, R.A., & Miller, J.M. (2002). A study of individual and situational antecedents of violent victimization. *Justice Quarterly, 19,* 159-180.

Schwartz, M.D., & Pitts, V.L. (1995). Exploring a feminist routine activities approach to explaining sexual assault. *Justice Quarterly, 12,* 9-31.

Sherman, L.S., Gartin, P.R., & Buerger, M.E. (1989). Hot spots of predatory crime: Routine activities and the criminology of place. *Criminology, 27,* 27-55.

Sheridan, L.P., Blaauw, E., & Davies, G.M. (2003). Stalking: Knowns and unknowns. *Trauma, Violence, & Abuse, 4,* 148-162.

Sheridan, L.P., & Grant, T. (2007). Is cyberstalking different? *Psychology, Crime & Law, 13,* 627-640.

Spelman, W. (1995). Criminal careers of public places. In J.E. Eck, & D. Weisburd (Eds.), *Crime and Place.* Crime prevention studies, vol. 4 (pp. 115-144). Monsey, NY: Criminal Justice Press.

Spitzberg, B.H. (2006). Preliminary development of a model and measure of computer-mediated communication (CMC) competence. *Journal of Computer-Mediated Communication, 11,* 629-666.

Spitzberg, B.H., & Cupach, W.R. (2007). The state of the art of stalking: Taking stock of the emerging literature. *Aggression and Violent Behavior, 12,* 64-86.

Spitzberg, B.H., & Hoobler, G. (2002). Cyberstalking and the technologies of interpersonal terrorism. *New Media & Society, 4,* 71-92.

Stewart, E.A., Elifson, K.W., & Sterk, C.E. (2004). Integrating the general theory of crime into an explanation of violent victimization among female offenders. *Justice Quarterly, 21,* 159-181.

Taylor, R.W., Fritsch, E.J., Liederbach, J., & Holt, T.J. (2010). *Digital Crime and Digital Terrorism* (2nd Edition.). Upper Saddle River, NJ: Pearson Prentice Hall.

Tewksbury, R., & Mustaine, E.E. (2003). College students' lifestyles and self-protective behaviors: Further considerations of the guardianship concept in routine activity theory. *Criminal Justice and Behavior, 30,* 302-327.

Tillyer, M.S., & Eck, J.E. (2009). Routine Activities. In J.M. Miller (Ed.). *21st Century Criminology: A Reference Handbook* (pp. 279-287). Thousand Oaks, CA: Sage.

Tjaden, P.G. (2009). Stalking policies and research in the United States: A twenty year retrospective. *European Journal on Criminal Policy Research, 15,* 261-278.

Tjaden P., & Thoennes, N. (1998). *Stalking in America: Findings from the National Violence Against Women Survey.* Washington D.C.: US Department of Justice: Bureau of Justice Statistics.

Townsley, M., Homel, R., & Chaseling, J. (2000). Repeat burglary victimisation: Spatial and temporal patterns. *Australian and New Zealand Journal of Criminology, 33,* 37-63.

van Wilsem, J. (2011). 'Bought it, but never got it': Assessing risk factors for online consumer fraud victimization. *European Sociological Review.* DOI: 10.1093/esr/jcr053

von Hentig, H. (1948). *The Criminal and His Victim.* New Haven, CT: Yale.

Wall, D.S. (2008). *Cybercrime: The Transformation of Crime in the Information Age.* Cambridge, UK: Polity Press.

Weisburd, D., Bushway, S., Lum, C., & Yang, S.M. (2004). Trajectories of crime at places: A longitudinal study of street segments in the city of Seattle. *Criminology, 42,* 283-322.

Weisburd, D., Maher, L., Sherman, L., Buerger, M., Cohn, E., & Petrosino, A. (1992). Contrasting crime general and crime specific theory: The case of hot spots of crime. In *Advances in Criminological Theory*, vol. 4 (pp. 45-70). New Brunswick, NJ: Transaction.

Wilcox, P., Jordan, C.E., & Pritchard, A.J. (2007). A multidimensional examination of campus safety: Victimization, perceptions of danger, worry about crime, and precautionary behavior among college women in the post-Clery era. *Crime & Delinquency, 53,* 219-254.

Wilcox, P., Land, K.C., & Hunt, S.A. (2003). *Criminal Circumstance: A Dynamic Multicontextual Criminal Opportunity Theory.* New York: Aldine de Gruyter.

Wilcox, P., Tillyer, M.S., & Fisher, B.S. (2009). Gendered opportunity?: School-based adolescent victimization. *Journal of Research in Crime and Delinquency, 46,* 245-269.

Wilcox Rountree, P., & Land, K.C. (1996). Burglary victimization, perceptions of crime risk, and routine activities: A multilevel analysis across Seattle neighborhoods and census tracts. *Journal of Research in Crime and Delinquency, 33,* 147-180.

Wilcox Rountree, P., Land, K. C., & Miethe, T. D. (1994). Macro-micro integration in the study of victimization: A hierarchical logistic model analysis across Seattle neighborhoods. *Criminology, 32,* 387-414.

Wolak, J., Finkelhor, D., Mitchell, K.J., & Ybarra, M.L. (2008). Online "predators" and their victims: Myths, realities, and implications for prevention and treatments. *American Psychologist, 63,* 111-128.

Wolfgang, M. E. (1958). *Patterns in Criminal Homicide.* Montclair, NJ: Patterson Smith.

Working to Halt Online Abuse (2009). *2008 Cyberstalking Statistics.* Retrieved September 26, 2009, from http://www.haltabuse.org/resources/stats/2008Statistics.pdf.

Wykes, M. (2007). Constructing crime: Culture, stalking, celebrity and cyber. *Crime Media Culture, 3,* 158-174.

Yar, M. (2005). The novelty of 'cybercrime': An assessment in light of routine activity theory. *European Journal of Criminology, 2,* 407-427.

Yar, M. (2006). *Cybercrime and Society.* Thousand Oaks, CA: Sage.

Index

AOL, 71-72, 95-96, 99, 101, 109, 111-116, 118, 121, 125, 133, 135, 175, 193, 199
Bivariate, 80, 95-96, 101, 103
Bocij, 5, 7-8, 10, 13, 16, 18-20, 69, 124, 201
Bossler, 5, 13, 15, 18, 21, 26-27, 40-42, 45, 47, 51-57, 72, 127-128, 202, 208
British Crime Survey, 1, 57
Bullying, 2
Capable guardianship, 30, 33, 38, 48, 54, 79
Choi, 47, 51-52, 54, 72, 128, 202
Clarke, 2, 30, 37, 47-50, 73-74, 132, 134, 139, 142, 202-205, 210
College students, 2, 3, 9, 15, 18-19, 23, 25-27, 30, 39, 41, 51-54, 56, 58, 61, 70, 73, 123, 126, 128, 130, 142-143, 149, 153, 201, 206, 207, 212
CRAVED, 37, 50, 74
Crime prevention, 3, 5, 41, 49, 50, 61, 132, 134-135, 202-203, 212
Crime triangle, 33, 38, 48
CyberAngels, 13

Cybercrimes, 2, 5, 20, 22, 47-50, 55, 59, 61, 73, 131-132, 139
Cyberlifestyle-Routine Activities Theory, 131
Cyberstalking, 2-28, 37, 40-41, 44-45, 49-51, 58-59, 61, 65, 67-69, 72, 74, 77-78, 81, 83-85, 89, 91, 93, 99, 105-106, 108-111, 117-119, 123-135, 137, 139-143, 145-146, 151, 153, 155, 201, 204, 208-209, 211-213
Dependent Variable, 15, 20
Deviant Lifestyles, 42
Dillman, 63-64, 67, 140, 203, 204
Eck, 33, 37, 47-49, 73, 127, 132, 134, 139-140, 142, 204-205, 212-214
Exposure, 29-33, 37-43, 53-55, 58, 70, 99, 106, 109, 118, 125-126, 130, 134-135, 137
Facebook, 9, 55, 127, 151, 153, 162, 165-166
Fear, 3, 6, 8-10, 15, 20-21, 23-24, 26, 146, 181, 184, 186, 188, 207

193

Felson, 1, 29, 32-33, 37-38, 131, 139, 203, 205
Finn, 7, 13, 15-16, 18, 20, 205
Fisher, 1, 3-6, 12-16, 18, 20, 24-29, 40-43, 50, 70, 74, 79-80, 126-128, 143, 202, 204-209, 212-213, 215
Gottfredson, 1, 42, 77-78, 119, 206-207, 211-212
Harassment, 2-5, 8, 11-12, 15-16, 18, 20-23, 27, 44, 52-54, 57, 80, 83-85, 89, 93, 99, 105-106, 108, 110, 117-118, 123-124, 126, 129, 145, 201-202, 204-205, 211
Henson, 4-10, 13, 29, 42, 45, 50, 55, 80, 149, 151, 153, 155, 189, 207, 212
Higgins, 5, 9, 18, 45, 47, 207, 209
Hindelang, 1, 30-32, 35, 37-38, 42, 79, 85, 207
Hirschi, 42, 77-78, 119, 206-207, 211
Holt, 5, 7, 13, 15, 18, 21, 26-27, 40-42, 45, 47, 51-55, 72, 127-128, 202, 208, 214
Identity fraud, 5, 7, 16, 65, 69, 83, 85, 89, 93, 105-106, 108-111, 118, 123, 125, 129-130, 208
Identity theft, 7-8, 20-21, 56, 212
Institutional Review Board, 62, 150, 189
Internet, 2, 6-7, 9, 11-13, 19-25, 28, 48, 52, 54-57, 64, 68, 124, 132, 134, 139, 142-143, 149, 151, 153, 155, 161, 201, 203-204, 211-212
Jerin, 13, 18, 20-21, 69, 208
Kraft, 15, 21, 23, 208

Lifestyle-exposure, 3, 28, 30-33, 38, 51-52, 61
Lifestyle-routine activities, 3, 5, 26-32, 37-45, 47, 50- 53, 55-59, 61, 67, 80-81, 83, 94, 106-107, 117-119, 123, 125, 128, 130, 133, 134, 141-142, 205, 206-208, 210, 212-214
Logistic regression, 81, 83, 107-109, 117, 125
Low self-control, 9, 41-45, 53, 59, 77-78, 83, 106, 117, 119, 129-130, 135, 140-141, 206-207, 213
Marcum, 5, 18, 47, 51, 54-55, 127, 209
Missing data, 65, 107, 201, 209
Motivated offender, 30, 33, 37-38
Multivariate, 81, 210
Mustaine, 4, 26-29, 40-44, 70, 72, 80, 126-128, 210, 214
National Crime Survey NCS, 1, 30
National Crime Victimization Survey, 14, 17, 24
Network Problems, 48
Networks, 2, 7, 48, 58, 71, 73, 99, 105, 110, 118, 125, 127-128, 131-132, 143, 149-151, 153, 155
NVAWS, 11-12, 18
Online Deviance, 75-77, 106, 117, 121, 128, 194, 199
Online exposure, 53, 58, 70, 99, 106, 109, 118, 125
Online guardianship, 52, 54, 58, 72, 105, 110, 118, 126, 130
Online proximity, 58, 73, 105, 128
Online target attractiveness, 58, 74

Index

Online Victimization, 85, 205, 207, 209
Opportunity, 1, 2, 5, 29-30, 33, 38, 43, 129, 133, 212, 215
Pilot Test, 68
Point biserial correlation coefficient, 80
Principle of homogamy, 32, 42, 53
Proximity, 4, 6, 10, 25, 37, 40-41, 44, 55, 58, 73, 79, 105-106, 110, 118, 127-130, 134-135, 137, 212
Pursuit, 83, 203
Race, 26, 30-31, 53, 57-58, 67, 79, 85, 89, 157, 196
Repeated pursuit, 3, 4, 16, 68
Response Rate, 63
Reyns, 1, 2, 6-7, 13-14, 29, 47-50, 56, 132, 134, 149, 151, 153, 155, 189, 205-207, 212
Risk Factors, 26, 125, 130
Risky Offline Activities, 80, 199
Routine activities, 5, 26-29, 32-33, 38-45, 48, 51-59, 61, 67, 73, 80, 94, 106, 119, 125-126, 129-132, 134, 139, 141-142, 202, 207-215
SCAREM, 50
Schreck, 29, 42-43, 45, 78-79, 213
Situational Crime Prevention, 137, 202-203
Social network, 44, 58, 67, 71-76, 80, 99, 126-127, 165-174, 189, 192-195, 207

Spitzberg, 4, 9, 13, 15-16, 18-20, 25, 93, 124, 203, 213-214
Stalking, 1-12, 14, 16-20, 22, 24-27, 40-41, 51, 68, 80, 93, 107, 123-124, 140-146, 190, 201, 203-206, 208, 210-215
Stalking laws, 3
Suitable target, 30, 33, 37-38
Super controllers, 139
Supplemental Victimization Survey, 24
Survey, 15-21, 52-57, 62-65, 67-72, 77-78, 80, 124, 126, 140-141, 149-151, 153, 155, 157, 165, 175, 180, 182, 184, 186, 189-190, 205
Systems problem, 48
Tailored Design Method, 63, 67, 203-204
Target attractiveness, 37, 40-41, 54-55, 58, 74-77, 106, 110, 119, 127-130
Threats, 4, 7-8, 16, 19, 44, 80-81, 83-84, 94, 99, 105-106, 110, 117, 124, 127, 129, 149
Tjaden, 4, 6, 18, 26, 93, 123-124, 214
University of Cincinnati, 62, 149-150, 207
VIVA, 37
Wilcox, 1, 4, 29-30, 38, 72, 79, 85, 207-208, 215
Working to Halt Online Abuse, 13, 23, 215
Yar, 5, 47, 131-132, 215

Zoomerang, 62